Edward Stratemeyer:
Creator of the Hardy Boys and Nancy Drew

WHO
WROTE
THAT?

WHO WROTE THAT?

Edward Stratemeyer:
Creator of the Hardy Boys and Nancy Drew

Brenda Lange

Foreword by
Kyle Zimmer

Chelsea House Publishers
Philadelphia

CHELSEA HOUSE PUBLISHERS

VP, NEW PRODUCT DEVELOPMENT   Sally Cheney
DIRECTOR OF PRODUCTION   Kim Shinners
CREATIVE MANAGER   Takeshi Takahashi
MANUFACTURING MANAGER   Diann Grasse

STAFF FOR EDWARD STRATEMEYER: CREATOR OF THE HARDY BOYS AND NANCY DREW

EDITOR Benjamin Kim
PICTURE RESEARCHER Pat Holl
PRODUCTION EDITOR Megan Emery
SERIES DESIGNER Keith Trego
LAYOUT 21st Century Publishing and Communications, Inc.

http://www.chelseahouse.com

First Printing

1 3 5 7 9 8 6 4 2

Library of Congress Cataloging-in-Publication Data

Lange, Brenda.
  Edward Stratemeyer / by Brenda Lange.
    p. cm. — (Who wrote that?)
Summary: A biography of the founder of the Stratemeyer Literary Syndicate, a publishing empire
that produced, in the early decades of the twentieth century, over 1400 adventure serial novels,
including the Hardy Boys and Nancy Drew series. Includes bibliographical references and index.
  ISBN 0-7910-7621-0
  1. Stratemeyer, Edward, 1862-1930—Juvenile literature. 2. Children's stories—Publishing
United States—History—20th century—Juvenile literature. 3. Authorship—Collaboration—
History—20th century—Juvenile literature. 4. Publishers and publishing—United States—
Biography—Juvenile literature. 5. Authors, American—20th century—Biography—Juvenile
literature. 6. Drew, Nancy (Fictitious character)—Juvenile literature. 7. Hardy Boys (Fictitious
characters)--Juvenile literature. 8. Stratemeyer Syndicate—Juvenile literature. [1. Stratemeyer,
Edward, 1862-1930. 2. Publishers and publishing. 3. Authors, American. 4. Authorship.
5.Stratemeyer Syndicate.] I. Title. II. Series.
  PS3537.T817Z76 2003
  813'.52—dc22
                                                                        2003019309

Table of Contents

FOREWORD BY
KYLE ZIMMER
PRESIDENT, FIRST BOOK

HUMANITY IS POWERED by stories. From our earliest days as thinking beings, we employed every available tool to tell each other stories. We danced, drew pictures on the walls of our caves, spoke, and sang. All of this extraordinary effort was designed to entertain, recount the news of the day, explain natural occurrences—and then gradually to build religious and cultural traditions and establish the common bonds and continuity that eventually formed civilizations. Stories are the most powerful force in the universe; they are the primary element that has distinguished our evolutionary path.

Our love of the story has not diminished with time. Enormous segments of societies are devoted to the art of storytelling. Book sales in the United States alone topped $26 billion last year; movie studios spend fortunes to create and promote stories; and the news industry is more pervasive in its presence than ever before.

There is no mystery to our fascination. Great stories are magic. They can introduce us to new cultures, or remind us of the nobility and failures of our own, inspire us to greatness or scare us to death, but above all, stories provide human insight on a level that is unavailable through any other source. In fact, stories connect each of us to the rest of humanity not just in our own time, but also throughout history.

This special magic of books is the greatest treasure that we can hand down from generation to generation. In fact, that spark in a child that comes from books became the motivation for the creation of my organization, First Book, a national literacy program with a simple mission: to provide new books to the most disadvantaged children. At present, First Book has been at work in hundreds of communities for over a decade. Every year children in need receive millions of books through our organization and millions more are provided through dedicated literacy institutions across the United States and around the world. In addition, groups of people dedicate themselves tirelessly to working with children to share reading and stories in every imaginable setting from schools to the streets. Of course, this Herculean effort serves many important goals. Literacy translates to productivity and employability in life and many other valid and even essential elements. But at the heart of this movement are people who love stories, love to read, and want desperately to ensure that no one misses the wonderful possibilities that reading provides.

When thinking about the importance of books, there is an overwhelming urge to cite the literary devotion of great minds. Some have written of the magnitude of the importance of literature. Amy Lowell, an American poet, captured the concept with her statement when she said, "Books are more than books. They are the life, the very heart and core of ages past, the reason why men lived and worked and died, the essence and quintessence of their lives." Others have spoken of their personal obsession with books, as in Thomas Jefferson's simple statement: "I live for books." But more compelling, perhaps, is the almost instinctive excitement in children for books and stories.

Throughout my years at First Book, I have heard truly extraordinary stories about the power of books in the lives of children. In one case, a homeless child, who had been bounced from one location to another, later resurfaced— and the only possession that he had fought to keep was the book he was given as part of a First Book distribution months earlier. More recently, I met a child who, upon receiving the book he wanted, flashed a big smile and said, "This is my big chance!" These snapshots reveal the true power of books and stories to give hope and change lives.

As these children grow up and continue to develop their love of reading, they will owe a profound debt to those volunteers who reached out to them—a debt that they may repay by reaching out to spark the next generation of readers. But there is a greater debt owed by all of us— a debt to the storytellers, the authors, who have bound us together, inspired our leaders, fueled our civilizations, and helped us put our children to sleep with their heads full of images and ideas.

WHO WROTE THAT? is a series of books dedicated to introducing us to a few of these incredible individuals. While we have almost always honored stories, we have not uniformly honored storytellers. In fact, some of the most important authors have toiled in complete obscurity throughout their lives or have been openly persecuted for the uncomfortable truths that they have laid before us. When confronted with the magnitude of their written work or perhaps the daily grind of our own, we can forget that writers are people. They struggle through the same daily indignities and dental appointments, and they experience the intense joy and bottomless despair that many of us do. Yet somehow they rise above it all to deliver a powerful thread that connects us all. It is a rare honor to have the opportunity that these books provide to share the lives of these extraordinary people. Enjoy.

In 1905, Edward Stratemeyer created the Stratemeyer Syndicate—a veritable "literature factory" in which hired ghostwriters produced mystery and adventure novels for children based on Stratemeyer's outlines. Stratemeyer would then edit and publish the works under different pseudonyms.

1

Talent, Luck, and Very Good Timing

"The reading capacity of the American adolescent is limitless. As oil had its Rockefeller, literature had its Stratemeyer."
—From a 1934 article in Fortune *magazine that called Stratemeyer's series books a "great natural resource."*

IT IS PROBABLY safe to say that most adults today are familiar with the intrepid girl detective Nancy Drew; the resourceful boy detectives, the Hardy Boys; and the inventive Tom Swift as characters in juvenile fiction series. Many millions grew up reading about their adventures, and millions of adolescents today still devour these books and others like them.

It also is probably true that few of those voracious readers know who created these books and thousands more. Edward Stratemeyer lived and died before most people alive today were born. But the characters he brought so vividly to life seemingly will never die.

Although his childhood was no more eventful than most of the late nineteenth century, Stratemeyer, through a series of fortuitous incidents and some amazingly good timing, found himself the head of an empire of sorts: what he called his Syndicate. Today, that word carries a far different connotation. But in the early decades of the twentieth century, the Stratemeyer Syndicate became synonymous with action-packed novels of mystery and adventure whose characters were immensely appealing to the average young boy and girl.

Adventure stories had always fascinated Stratemeyer. So it is no wonder his heroes and heroines always managed to get themselves into dangerous situations, but then also were able to get themselves out, rising above challenges that would thwart the average teenager, but merely slowing these characters down for a time.

Edward Stratemeyer was known as a private person, and no comprehensive biography of him has ever been written. He was known to sometimes "craft" the truth to make himself sound better to the public. For example, he often stressed the high moral tone of his books, although many of his dime novels were known for their inherent criminal element—with characters who drank, smoked, gambled, and more—sensational stuff for the early part of the twentieth century. His stories for women were highly romanticized and syrupy sweet. It is questionable, though, whether they could be considered "instructive," as he often described his work.

In trying to describe the many facets of Stratemeyer's character, one researcher calls him a "shrewd capitalist who adapted himself to the needs of whatever marketplace he could work in." Perhaps he simply matured and moved on to a different place in his life, a place in which he wasn't as proud of his earlier, more sensationalistic work. Now that he was the owner of a successful publishing empire—someone who held his writers to a high moral code—perhaps he felt the need to rewrite his life story to fit his new self-image.

In addition to authoring a number of books in various series, he wrote the outlines of others for most of his ghostwriters. Many of these series were owned outright by Stratemeyer, since he bought all rights from the writers or publishers. He had learned early in his career that there was money to be made in reselling his work, not something you could do without owning the copyright.

According to several accounts, Stratemeyer was a stern disciplinarian both at home with his wife and two daughters and in his Manhattan office with his cadre of writers. Leslie McFarlane, one of Stratemeyer's top ghostwriters, wrote in his autobigraphy that Stratemeyer had little sense of humor with his employees and never showed praise or lightheartedness.

McFarlane wrote that Stratemeyer was "best and most publicly known for placing his own success at the summit of his priorities. He demonstrated a terrible swift sword whenever he thought anyone was infringing on his territory." This aspect of his personality can be seen in the story of a young writer who had written some parodies of the Rover Boys, arguably Stratemeyer's best-loved series. Stratemeyer not only threatened to sue the writer, but also threatened to throw him out of his office window, should he ever come there.

The world—especially the adolescent world—was ready for the characters that Stratemeyer and the writers of his

Syndicate were developing. New discoveries were being made daily, and young people longed to be a part of them. Through Dick, Tom, and Sam Rover; Tom Swift; and Frank and Joe Hardy, they could move outside their own small world into a larger one filled with adventure. Following a prescribed formula and an outline penned by Stratemeyer, his ghostwriters could each churn out a book every four to six weeks. For $50 to $250, these authors signed away all rights and agreed never to divulge their identities. Within six years of the inception of the syndicate, twenty-two different series were in progress. Three to five new volumes within each series were published annually, making Edward Stratemeyer a rich man.

Many adults didn't quite understand the allure of a Stratemeyer book, but their children knew better. Critics of the Syndicate formula included teachers, librarians, parents, and even a high-ranking Boy Scout official. Some women in Portland, Oregon, even staged protests in bookstores, urging young boys to boycott the books. Newspaper editorials and

Did you know...

During Stratemeyer's lifetime, he frequently corresponded with artists and commissioned art for both his personal books and those produced by his Syndicate. After his death in May 1930, the decisions regarding artwork were largely left to the publishers. As cultural forces changed, so did the illustrations, which were updated along with the prose to keep the series fresh and appealing to new generations.

other articles urged parents to be on the lookout for the negative behaviors these books could encourage.

But Stratemeyer had found his niche. He said, "Any writer who has the young for an audience can snap his fingers at all the critics." And it was true. By 1926 a library survey found that Tom Swift books were on 98 percent of their young readers' reading lists. Ironically, although he had made millions through his adventure novels, he remained relatively unknown until the "birth" of his most enduring heroine near the end of his life—Nancy Drew.

In 1929, with the success of the Hardy Boys series, Stratemeyer felt the time was right for a similar series about a girl. He created a young "everywoman"—an American ideal—with blond hair and blue eyes, unafraid, determined, and curious. She represented just who every adolescent girl imagined herself to be.

Stratemeyer wrote the outlines for the first three books of the series about this girl detective and hired Mildred Wirt, who had first written for the Syndicate while a journalism student at the University of Iowa, to write the first three Nancy Drew volumes. When Stratemeyer first read the books, he felt she had made Nancy too "fresh and aggressive." Apparently, his publisher, Grosset & Dunlap, disagreed and bought the books as Wirt had written them. Unfortunately, Stratemeyer died about a month before the first one was published, never seeing what a monumental success the series would become.

Although the Syndicate's founder was no longer alive, his characters continued to live through the guidance of his daughters, Harriet and Edna, and the contract writers they continued to employ.

Young Americans had found their heroes and heroines and they were here to stay.

GOLDEN DAYS

FOR BOYS AND GIRLS.

(Entered according to Act of Congress, in the year 1889, by James Elverson, in the Office of the Librarian of Congress, at Washington, D. C.

VOL. X.   JAMES ELVERSON, N. W. corner Ninth   PHILADELPHIA, NOVEMBER 2, 1889.   TERMS: $3.00 PER ANNUM, IN ADVANCE.   No. 49.
Publisher, and Spruce Sts.

VICTOR HORTON'S IDEA.

BY EDWARD STRATEMEYER.

CHAPTER I.

GREAT NEWS.

It was indeed great news for the Belmont boys. A real city show, and a double one, too, was to give an exhibition at the town hall.

These wonderful tidings had been circulated by means of the following poster, conspicuously displayed throughout the neighborhood:

COMING! COMING! COMING!

Zwing's World-Famous Uncle Tom's Cabin and Humpty Dumpty Pantomime Troop.

The strongest combination extant! Two distinct companies in one grand double bill of unapproachable excellence! The savage, untamed Siberian bloodhound Leo! The comical donkey Wisdom! The favorite South Carolina Jubilee Shouters! The greatest of all great Clowns, Tim Dicks! The Royal Gold Cornet Band!

Belmont Hall, Monday, November 3.

Admission, 25 cents. Reserved seats extra. Doors open at 7 P. M. Performance at 8.

N. B.—Don't fail to hear the open-air concert before the opening of the doors.

No wonder that the feelings of the young folks were stirred to their deepest depths. Outside of the annual school exhibitions during holiday week, no shows had occurred for full three years. And this—this was to be so grand and immense! Oh, but wasn't it just "boss!" Half the boys hugged themselves thinking about it.

Among the number was Victor Horton, the son of a prosperous farmer, whose broad acres lay a mile from the township centre.

Victor was fifteen years old, naturally bright and lively, and if he had not held so high an opinion of himself, he would have been a first-rate lad.

Besides being conceited, Victor was dissatisfied with the quietness of country life. He longed to go forth into the great world and achieve fame and fortune.

Now, though this idea is often a very laudable one, it was not so in the present instance. Victor's idea upon the subject had been gathered wholly from the pages of numerous dime novels and disreputable story-papers loaned him by his particular crony, Sam Wilson, and was, therefore, of a deceptive and unsubstantial nature, and likely to do more harm than good.

But Victor was not aware of this, and it is quite probable that he would not have believed it, had he been told. It is my purpose to relate what his idea led to, and how the complicated affair terminated.

It was early morning of the day upon which the exhibition was to be given. Victor stood in a crowd of boys, waiting for Mr. Walner, the schoolmaster, to arrive and open school.

"Tell you what, boys," Sam Wilson was saying, as he held up one of the show-bills, "my idea is that it's rattling good, and no mistake."

"I believe you," agreed Billy Parsons, "and you can just bet I won't miss it, either."

These remarks worried Victor. The truth was that though he had set his heart upon going, he was by no means sure of gaining the required permission.

Mr. Horton was a strict man. He had begun life poor, and now, when the fruits of labor were accumulated around him, he did not believe in allowing money to slip away too easily. He was not close-fisted, only economical—a habit which his only son sadly misconstrued as a mere restraint upon personal liberty.

"Of course you will go, Vic?" continued Sam.

His "of course" meant a good deal to Victor. It was taken for granted, then, that he would go, and so it would never do to admit that permission must first be obtained.

"Oh, of course," he replied, loftily.

"Then stop at my house at half-past six, and we'll go together," said his crony. "We want to hear the open-air concert, you know."

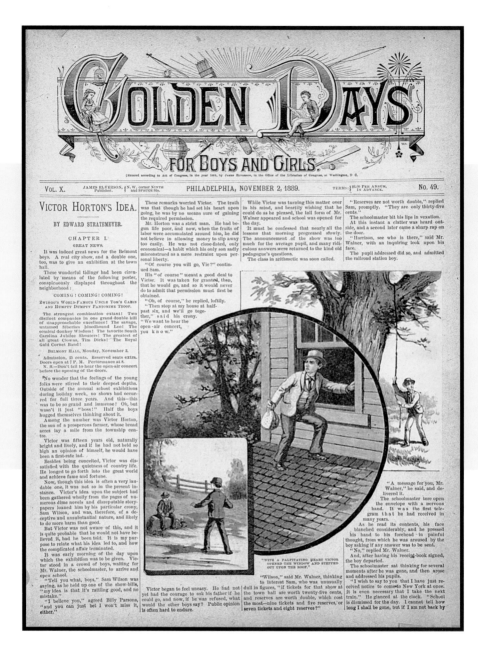

"With a palpitating heart Victor opened the window and stepped out upon the roof."

Victor began to feel uneasy. He had not yet had the courage to ask his father if he could go, and now, if he was refused, what would the other boys say? Public opinion is often hard to endure.

While Victor was turning this matter over in his mind, and heartily wishing that he could do as he pleased, the tall form of Mr. Walner appeared and school was opened for the day.

It must be confessed that nearly all the lessons that morning progressed slowly. The announcement of the show was too much for the average pupil, and many ridiculous answers were returned to the kind old pedagogue's questions.

The class in arithmetic was soon called.

"Wilson," said Mr. Walner, thinking to interest Sam, who was unusually dull in figures, "if tickets for that show at the town hall are worth twenty-five cents, and reserves are worth double, which cost the most—nine tickets and five reserves, or seven tickets and eight reserves?"

"Reserves are not worth double," replied Sam, promptly. "They are only thirty-five cents."

The schoolmaster bit his lips in vexation.

At this instant a clatter was heard outside, and a second later came a sharp rap on the door.

"Harrison, see who is there," said Mr. Walner, with an inquiring look upon his face.

The pupil addressed did so, and admitted the railroad station boy.

"A message for you, Mr. Walner," he said, and he delivered it.

The schoolmaster tore open the envelope with a nervous hand. It was the first telegram that he had received in many years.

As he read its contents, his face blanched considerably, and he pressed his hand to his forehead in painful thought, from which he was aroused by the boy asking if any answer was to be sent.

"No," replied Mr. Walner.

And, after having his receipt-book signed, the boy departed.

The schoolmaster sat thinking for several moments after he was gone, and then arose and addressed his pupils.

"I wish to say to you that I have just received notice to come to New York at once. It is even necessary that I take the next train." He glanced at the clock. "School is dismissed for the day. I cannot tell how long I shall be gone, but if I am not back by

At twenty-seven, Stratemeyer penned his first published work, "Victor Horton's Idea," on a roll of brown wrapping paper. The story was purchased by the Philadelphia boys' magazine Golden Days for Boys and Girls for $75 and marked a turning point in Stratemeyer's career, showing him that a living could be made from literature.

2

Who Was Edward Stratemeyer?

EDWARD STRATEMEYER WAS a first-generation American. He was born in Elizabeth, New Jersey, on October 4, 1862, to two German immigrants. His father, Henry Julius Stratemeyer, crossed the Atlantic in 1837 and in 1849 traveled to San Francisco during the great gold rush. When his brother George died in 1854, Henry returned to New Jersey to settle his estate. Shortly thereafter, he and his sister-in-law, Anna Siegel, married and eventually had three children. Anna had previously had three children with George. Edward was the youngest of the six sibling-cousins.

According to all reports, Edward was raised in a strict,

German-American home with Victorian attitudes and expectations. His later strict upbringing of his own children and management of his business affairs reflected that childhood. Edward attended school in Elizabeth and graduated from Public School No. 3 at age sixteen. According to researcher and author, James D. Keeline, he was valedictorian of his three-student graduating class and gave a speech titled, "Experience is the school where man learns wisdom."

Nearly as soon as he learned to read, Edward also began writing short stories. His favorite authors were Horatio Alger, Jr. and Oliver Optic (pseudonym for William T. Adams) who wrote adventure stories for boys with strong, conservative, and moral overtones. Edward published a small newspaper, *Our Friend*, and story paper, *The Young American*, making a little money off the sale of advertisements. (Story papers were short magazines with fiction, puzzles, and ads). He published a four-page booklet called *That Bottle of Vinegar* in 1877 and a thirty-two-page booklet titled *The Tale of a Lumberman* that tells of a trip into the woods of Maine. He also wrote and published some short magazine stories.

Henry Stratemeyer wasn't very supportive of his youngest son's aspirations to become a writer and discouraged him from continuing to work toward a career as a writer. He didn't feel it was an appropriate way for a man to make a living and provide for his family. Edward's father owned and operated a tobacco shop, in which his older brothers/cousins also worked. Eventually, one brother bought his own stationery store, and Edward went to work for him. But he never stopped writing in his free time. During this time, Edward wrote for magazines and published two eight-page story papers containing short stories, serialized longer pieces, jokes, puzzles, and ads. He also began the practice of writing under a pseudonym. Some of his earliest pen names were Ed Ward, Robert Rollic, and Will Smith. Only bits and pieces of his writing remain from the early 1880s—including song lyrics, some poetry, short story fragments, a romance, and librettos for two operettas. As the decade progressed, he continued to move closer to success.

The turning point came for Edward, according to an anecdote he often told, during a slow business day in his brother's store. He sat down with a roll of brown wrapping paper and proceeded to write out a long adventure story. It was reportedly about 18,000 words, making it a very long roll of paper. He submitted the story, "Victor Horton's Idea," to a Philadelphia boys' magazine called *Golden Days for Boys and Girls.* The magazine bought the story for the astonishing sum of $75— about six times what he was making each week, and, at the age of twenty-seven, Edward was on his way.

Ironically, his father had urged Edward to forget about that particular story, admonishing him for "wasting his time" and not doing "something more useful," Stratemeyer recounted in a 1917 interview with the *Newark Sunday Call.* The reporter wrote: "The story of a successful writer's first accepted story possesses a certain fascination for his admirers that nothing else quite equals." Edward was quoted as saying: "If I hadn't wanted to use the money, I would have framed that check! I took it uptown where my father was in business and found him reading his newspaper. 'They paid me this for writing a story,' I explained proudly. 'Paid you that for writing a story?' repeated my father. 'Well, you'd better write a lot more of them!'"

With or without his father's encouragement, it's likely that Edward would have continued his writing career. In the following years, he submitted more stories to *Golden Days* and then was hired there as an associate editor for $20 a week.

Two years later, Edward opened his own stationery shop in Newark, New Jersey, all the while continuing to write and publish short stories and dime novels, so called because they sold for 10¢ each. In 1891, he married fellow writer Magdalene (Lena) Baker Van Camp. Shortly after their marriage, his father died. The following December, the couple had their first child, Harriet. A second daughter, Edna, was born in May 1895. Between the births of his two daughters, he wrote and sold his first book, *Richard Dare's Venture*, published by Merriam in 1895.

At this point, Edward was an associate editor of *Young Sports of America*—later changed to *Young People of America*—to which he contributed short stories and serialized longer pieces. Stratemeyer always tried to buy back the copyrights to his stories—wisely as it turned out in the case of *Young People*

Did you know...

"As a boy . . . I had quite a library, including many of Optic's and Alger's books. At seven or eight, when I was reading them I said: 'If I could only write books like that I'd be the happiest person on earth.'"

—Edward Stratemeyer,
Newark Evening News, June 4, 1927.

Edward's obituary in the *New York Times* explained his choice of the pseudonym Arthur M. Winfield for his Rover Boys series: "Arthur almost rhymed with author; 'M' stood for the million copies of his books he hoped to see published; and Winfield referred to the success he wanted in his chosen profession."

of America. The magazine went out of business shortly after changing its name, but Stratemeyer was able to take his stories they had printed and republish them. He made the final move toward becoming a full-time author and publisher when he sold his stationery store and began publishing a story paper he named *Bright Days.* In this publication, he republished many of his previously printed stories. He also was working as an editor at *Street & Smith* where he published sixteen dime novels in three years and was fortunate to work with Upton Sinclair, well-known later as the author of *The Jungle.*

The depression of 1897 hit the publishing industry hard, and many magazines and papers went out of business. Edward tried another venture, the Comrades Publishing Company, a cooperative for his writing friends who were having a hard time finding markets for their work. Unfortunately, this too failed. But Stratemeyer was about to get a lucky break by being in the right place at the right time.

The year was 1898 and Lee & Shepard Publishers of Boston had just bought Stratemeyer's new adventure novel about two boys on a United States battleship. When the Spanish-American War broke out, the editor at Lee & Shepard asked Edward to make a few changes to his manuscript to make it more topical. Edward agreed, and *Under Dewey at Manila or The War Fortunes of a Castaway* was published in July of that year. It was the first book in his proposed Old Glory series and went through four printings, selling 6,000 copies by Christmas. In the subsequent books of the series, the heroes of that first novel later charged up San Juan Hill with Teddy Roosevelt and fought in the jungles of Luzon.

William T. Adams, one of Edward's favorite childhood authors, had been a star at Lee & Shepard for years and died just before Edward's big break with the Old Glory series' premiere novel. An editor at that publishing company was asked in an interview ". . .who is there among the young writers of juvenile stories to take the place so long filled by the late Oliver Optic [Adams]?" He replied, "I don't know, unless it is Edward Stratemeyer." Less than a year later, this prophetic statement proved true. Edward was hired to write the final volume in Optic's Blue and Grey on Land series, *An Undivided Union* published by Lee & Shepard in 1899.

That same year, Edward got another chance to write in the guise of one of his boyhood heroes. Over the years, he and Horatio Alger, Jr., had become good friends. When Alger's health began to decline in 1898, he offered to sell some of his unfinished manuscripts to Edward to finish and publish. After Alger's death, Edward did indeed purchase several manuscripts, plays, and a scrapbook of short stories from Alger's sister. He paid up to $150 for each, agreed to publish them under Alger's name, and was allowed to insert the line "completed by Arthur M. Winfield" in each book. Because Alger was so well-established, Edward was able to get advances on the finished work, selling to publishers who knew and respected Alger. This was an example of Edward's fine business sense. He was paid more for each advance than he had paid Alger's sister for the work in the first place.

At the same time—around the turn of the century—Stratemeyer contracted with a new publishing company in Rahway, New Jersey, to sell edited reprints of his Rover Boys Series for Young Americans, later known simply as The Rover Boys, which some sources say was his favorite series, and to which he continued to add volumes through 1926.

Stratemeyer's love of reading and writing juvenile adventure fiction, his keen business instincts, and fortuitous timing helped make him one of the most successful writers, publishers, and entrepreneurs of the past century. If he had simply continued to pen short magazine stories, churn out dime novels, and work as an editor, he may have slipped into obscurity, making little more than that first $75 per story. But through the writing of these early pieces, he developed an understanding for what young readers wanted and a formula for success that would define what adolescents would read into the twenty-first century.

Howard Garis, one of the Stratemeyer Syndicate's most prolific writers, wrote more than 300 books between 1905 and 1935, including the majority of the 38-volume Tom Swift series.

3

The Stratemeyer Literary Syndicate

EDWARD STRATEMEYER'S EARLIEST works may be remembered today only by collectors and the very old, but they laid the groundwork for the series and characters that followed. He was amazingly prolific, churning out dozens of volumes, articles, and stories every year. But even someone as organized and self-motivated as he was can write only so many words each day. The solution to this dilemma was the Stratemeyer Literary Syndicate, what one researcher has called "a veritable literary factory." His innovative approach to series fiction writing took the publishing industry by storm.

Stratemeyer worked from 9 to 5 every day in his Manhattan office, a short commute from his Newark, New Jersey, home. It was his practice to dictate 7,500 words a day. Over time, he realized that, even though he wrote diligently every day, producing more pages than most writers, his rich imagination was outpacing his ability to write. By 1905, he had conceived of a master plan that would shape the rest of his life and literary history.

When he formalized his Syndicate, he did so under a set of rules and regulations. His insistence on this formal method is what ensured his success. First, he took his story ideas and crafted them into detailed outlines, including characterizations, plot, and setting. Then he hired writers with whom he had worked before or who answered his ads. Many of these ghostwriters were journalists or former reporters. The writer would then flesh out the outline, creating a complete novel—of about 220 pages—within four to six weeks. Stratemeyer then would edit the work and send it off to the publisher. Usually no more than forty days passed from the story's conception to a finished manuscript. The publishing world at this time was expanding rapidly and needed a constant stream of product to continue to grow. The Syndicate met that demand.

Stratemeyer worked with several publishing companies but primarily with Grosset & Dunlap. Sometimes he would sell the proposal before he outlined the story, but often it was the finished version that was sold.

By all accounts, Stratemeyer was methodical and conscientious in his management of the Syndicate. His rules were law, and the writers who worked for him followed them. Possibly the most important rule was that these authors were to remain anonymous ghostwriters, never divulging their true identities. Stratemeyer felt that the name of the author on the cover of a book was almost as important as what appeared inside. Since each writer followed Stratemeyer's scrupulously written outlines, the writing was similar in tone and substance, and giving each series one "author" helped in continuity and minimized confusion among readers.

For example, Franklin W. Dixon was the sole author of the Hardy Boys series. But there was no such person. This series was conceived by Stratemeyer and written by about twenty different writers. The name Carolyn Keene later became synonymous with the Nancy Drew series, but again, the adventures of the famous girl sleuth were written by about eighteen writers, including Stratemeyer's daughter, Harriet. About thirteen people wrote as Laura Lee Hope, the author of the Bobbsey Twins.

The use of pseudonyms disguised the fact that different writers were used, creating a specific identity for the author of each series. Even when the real writer inevitably moved on to other work or died, the pen name remained associated with the series. If a series was successful, the pen name from that series could be used to launch another series by the same author. This was the case, for instance, with the Rover Boys and Putnam Hall series, both of which were written by Arthur M. Winfield, aka Edward Stratemeyer. To maintain this illusion of continuity, even among his own stable of writers, it is said that Stratemeyer staggered appointments with his authors, so none would ever meet and have the chance to compare notes.

His fictitious authors had full lives created by the pub-lisher's publicity department. Often they were promoted as experts in the subject area about which they wrote. For example, Margaret Penrose, author of the Motor Girls series was promoted in this way: "Besides being an able writer . . . she is an expert automobilist." And Lester Chadwick, author of Baseball Joe, "has played on the diamond and on the gridiron himself." For marketing purposes, it was felt that having certified "experts" writing these books would boost sales.

The first series published by the Syndicate was the Bobbsey Twins, the first volume appearing in 1904, just before Stratemeyer formalized the Syndicate's operation. The Bobbsey Twins went on to become one of its most successful, lasting until the early 1990s, with a total of ninety-six volumes published. Within the next seven years, Stratemeyer introduced at least ten new series including Tom Swift, the Motor Boys, the Motor Girls, and Ruth Fielding.

To maintain order and ensure productivity, Stratemeyer established other rules. Each new series was introduced with a "breeder set" of books: the first three books written and published at about the same time were used to build an audience and gauge its reaction. If this trio sold well, then additional books would be planned for that particular series. Carol

Did you know...

In 1900, Stratemeyer wrote, "I have made up my mind to stick to juveniles, not only under my own name, but under my nom-de-plumes, and I am studying that market in all of its conditions and am also studying the wants of the publishers, with a view to supplying the latter not alone with stories of my own, but also the stories of others, written under my direction, on subjects which I feel will attract sales."

Billman, author of *The Secret of the Stratemeyer Syndicate: Nancy Drew, The Hardy Boys and the Million Dollar Fiction Factory*, calls this system of production and promotion the "pearl necklace" system. If every series is imagined as a chain, or pearl necklace, then each individual title is a pearl in that necklace. To keep the chain intact, at the beginning of each book earlier books in the series are recounted and toward the end of the book, the next "pearl" or title in the series is alluded to.

Stratemeyer felt that such hindsight and foresight enabled new readers to 'catch up' with the actions of the hero and ensured that readers would come back for more exciting adventures in upcoming books.

If a series continued to be popular, sometimes a 'second generation' of books was developed. For example, Tom Swift eventually led to the publication of Tom Swift Jr. in 1954. By the 1920s, the Rover Boys settled down, got married, and had sons of their own, whose adventures picked up where their fathers' had left off.

Of course, there were many series that were allowed to die off. Not many will remember the Grammar School Boys, the Submarine Chums, or Aunt Jane's Nieces, even though the last series was written by L. Frank Baum, the author of the Oz books. The White Ribbon Boys, introduced in 1915, which was about "the great modern movement for temperance," sank into oblivion, as did the Flyaways, a fantasy series launched in 1925. Years later, the Tolivers, a 1967 adventure series about a black family, lasted only one year. Occasionally, Stratemeyer was able to take a failed series and rework it into one that worked. This is just what happened with the Up and Doing series which was introduced in 1912 and later became the Fairview Boys.

Each series developed signature elements. According to

a 1992 *Smithsonian* article, "The Rover Boys developed a talent for having their luggage stolen. The Hardy Boys were adept at exploring claustrophobic spaces like caves, old forts, and deserted cabins. Nancy Drew, though a skilled pilot, driver, and boat captain, could never seem to find a vehicle without a jammed throttle, flat tire, bum steering, or faulty brakes." There were rules about style, structure, plot, characterization, and setting, all of which created a comfortable familiarity to all the novels.

The settings for Stratemeyer's books were similar in nature. Most of the stories took place in quiet, small towns whose peacefulness was just a façade. Under the surface, there flowed an undercurrent of thieves, kidnappers, and other "bad" guys. In addition, these little towns seemed to have the worst weather imaginable! Thunderstorms were as common as the villains. But, no matter the intervening mishaps and adventures, the heroes and heroines always managed to return to their homes, safe and sound, where their respective adult authority figures were waiting to congratulate them on a job well done.

Stratemeyer's idea for writing series books wasn't a new one, but he capitalized on the success of those who came before him. He didn't just mimic the style of his predecessors, however, and he was conscious of writing "up-to-date action and characters who enjoyed the freedoms and privileges of a new era," wrote Billman. The lack of adult supervision was one of his largest departures from books of the same genre of an earlier generation. As Billman notes, "Stratemeyer's fiction depicted freewheeling youth who lived in the present and sported such contemporary luxury items as motor boats, automobiles, motorcycles, or airplanes." He adhered to a certain moral code, but that code was overshadowed by the adventure and suspense of the story.

Some felt that Stratemeyer was stingy, paying his ghost-writers only about $50 to $250 per book for which they gave up all rights, although he did pay promptly. But it is also documented that he was fair and often generous in his treatment of his employees. According to the Syndicate's accounting records, he gave some of his writers annual bonuses, he always gave Christmas bonuses. He was a philanthropist, donating money to Helen Keller's home for blind children, among others, and he mentored aspiring writers. Leslie McFarlane, one of the Syndicate's primary writers, wrote in his autobiography, *The Ghost of the Hardy Boys*, that Stratemeyer provided for his ghostwriters in his will, leaving them "a sum equal to a percentage of what they'd earned from him." McFarlane also noted that Stratemeyer sent him a check when each of his children was born. "He had his kind side," he wrote.

By all accounts, Stratemeyer was as shy and protective of his private life as he was successful as a businessman and prolific as an author. He disliked public speaking, and although in demand by youth organizations, he said he "preferred to communicate with his young friends through letters and in the prefaces of his books." His younger daughter, Edna, wrote in a letter that her father enjoyed quiet vacations where he found the time to fish, drive in the country, and people-watch—a respite from his demanding daily work schedule. He also enjoyed taking his family on vacations in Ocean Grove and Atlantic City, New Jersey, and traveling cross-country to Seattle, Washington; Yellowstone Park in Wyoming; the Canadian Rockies; and California.

His home was a comfortable place to be, thanks to the success of the Syndicate. His wife had a maid and cook and there were nurses for the children. The Stratemeyers owned a player piano, Victrola (phonograph), and telephone.

As an automobile enthusiast, Stratemeyer owned several touring cars in which he and his wife loved to drive.

Dr. Ilana Nash, another Stratemeyer scholar, writes about Stratemeyer's love of baseball, especially the New York Giants and their pitcher, Christy Mathewson. She writes, "This choice is revealing, for it tells us something of Stratemeyer's taste in heroes. Christy Mathewson, although hardly known today, was not only a Hall of Fame-ranking ball player, but also renowned for being an honest, gentlemanly, decent person." Stratemeyer also admired American presidents, writing biographies and stories about McKinley, Theodore Roosevelt, and Washington.

Although he worked hard for his success, the level of that success took him by surprise. Just prior to the publication of the fifteenth title in the Rover Boys series, Stratemeyer wrote, "Twelve years ago the line was started with the publication of the first three stories . . . I earnestly hoped that the young people would like the tales, but never did I anticipate the tremendously enthusiastic welcome which was given to the volumes from the start, nor the steady sales, ever increasing, which have accompanied the series up to the present time."

Stratemeyer exhibited something of a sixth sense when it came to the business end of his writing venture. In addition to putting into place the rules of operation that would keep the writers producing smoothly, he was able to quickly assess the popularity of any given series and make the correct decision about whether to continue it or not. Also, the year after forming the Syndicate, he was able to convince Cupples & Leon, the publisher of his Motor Boys series, to sell the books as "fifty-centers" or about half of what the novels usually sold for. He accurately predicted that the company would more than make up for any lost revenue in increased sales.

Howard R. Garis was one of the first writers to join the

Syndicate, proving himself over the years to be one of its most prolific writers and a good friend to Stratemeyer. He wrote more than 300 books between 1905 and 1935. Originally a reporter for the *Newark Evening News*, he also wrote books under his own name in his spare time. As Victor Appleton, he earned a reputation as the author of the Tom Swift series. He also created the Uncle Wiggily character, loved by so many young children. Lilian Garis, Howard's wife and fellow newspaper reporter, wrote volumes in several series, including the Bobbsey Twins and the Outdoor Girls. Working for the Syndicate was a Garis family affair: their children Roger and Cleo also worked for Stratemeyer years later.

The Stratemeyer Syndicate relied on several publishing companies to publish its various series. Chatterton-Peck was its original publisher, but around 1907 Stratemeyer became unhappy with some of their methods and entered into an agreement with Grosset & Dunlap for many subsequent series. As the twentieth century passed, competitors to Stratemeyer's operation appeared. Grosset & Dunlap even published other mystery/suspense/adventure novels for young adults, including the Tom Slade Scout series by Percy Keese Fitzhugh. The competition didn't seem to hurt Stratemeyer, however. Overall, the Stratemeyer Syndicate produced more than 1,400 series books that were written by 100 ghostwriters under about 75 different pseudonyms.

Stratemeyer opened all his books with an introductory letter he usually began as "My Dear Lads," or "Young Friends." These letters foreshadowed the plot and was both a way to introduce the novel and bring new readers up to speed. This habit began with his first book, *Under Dewey at Manila, or The War Fortunes of a Castaway,* a historical book about the Spanish-American War. He opened it with an explanation of his reasons for writing the book: ". . . to present to young readers a simple and straightforward statement concerning the several causes leading up to the war with Spain and . . . to tell the haps and mishaps of a sturdy conscientious American lad, of good moral character and honest Christian aim, who, compelled through the force of circumstances to make his own way in the world, becomes a sailor boy, a castaway, and then a gunner's assistant on the flagship *Olympia*." Although this language sounds stilted today, it attracted thousands of readers.

After a time, when the Syndicate was at its peak, Stratemeyer devoted himself totally to the business, marketing, and publicity aspects of it, leaving the writing to others.

As for the girls' series, as the twentieth century moved forward, so did the female lead characters. They became increasingly independent, resourceful, and able to triumph over adversities outside the home. These character traits were in direct contrast to the young women in the novels of the late 1800s, which focused on the suffering and hardships of young women who had to prevail over domestic problems, but were rarely seen involved in much of any substance outside the home. They were often sentimental and melodramatic. Stratemeyer's young women were tomboys who climbed trees and got into trouble right alongside the boys in all kinds of suspenseful situations. Or they led a double life, as career girl and sleuth, as socialite and sleuth, and so on. They were allowed to move out of domestic drudgery and attend boarding schools and go to work, moving out into the world around them, just like their male counterparts.

The Syndicate's adventure series can be broken down into several categories or subgenres, whose differences are found in the plot rather than in the category. One can choose school and sports novels, science, war stories, or mystery. The books become easily recognizable using these basic formulas. For example, Nancy Drew and Hardy Boys mystery novels always featured the fast action of the chase, breaking of codes, stereotypical heroes and villains, and, of course, the clues that are almost too good to be true: the footprints and bloodstains are always fresh! And last but not least, justice always prevails in the end.

Andrew Svenson joined the Syndicate as a full-time writer in 1948 and developed such series as The Happy Hollisters, The Bret King, and The Tolliver Family.

4

Critical Failure, Commercial Success

EDWARD STRATEMEYER AND his writers were busy churning out dozens of books a year. Not only was Stratemeyer responsible for outlining books in each series, writing some of them, hiring ghostwriters, and editing the finished product, but he soon spent most of his time creating characters and plot lines that would sell, finding publishers, marketing the books, and managing all the business of the Syndicate. It wasn't an easy job. The Stratemeyer Syndicate was number one in the world of adolescent adventure serial novels, and the kids loved them.

Children's fiction was a fairly new phenomenon, tracing its roots back to the mid-1800s. After the Civil War, most literature for juveniles followed one formula: an ordinary boy overcame many obstacles to achieve success. Stratemeyer relied on authors from that era for inspiration for his heroes and heroines. The Five Little Peppers books and Louisa May Alcott's stories directly influenced his series for girls and younger readers of both sexes such as the Bobbsey Twins and Dorothy Dale, just as the books of Horatio Alger and Oliver Optic (William T. Adams) influenced his boys' books. However, he didn't just mimic their styles. He was careful to update his plots, characters, and settings to make the stories more appealing to contemporary adolescents. Although Stratemeyer's idea for writing series books wasn't original, he capitalized on its success. In turn, his work and that of his ghostwriters laid the foundation for today's successful authors of series books in mystery, adventure, and romance.

When Stratemeyer was young, children were thought of as little adults. They went straight from childhood to adulthood in dress, behavior, and expectations. There was no such thing as a teenager. In the cities, children worked in factories; in the country, they worked on farms. Soon they had families of their own. By the first years of the twentieth century, however, with the economy on an upswing and social consciousness being raised, childhood lasted longer, creating a new stage—adolescence.

Adolescence as a stage of life came about during the height of the popularity of the books produced by the Stratemeyer Syndicate. With new child-labor laws in place and compulsory education until age sixteen, youngsters had more free time, with none of the technological advances of the second half of the century to fill it—no computers, television, or even radio in the beginning. Stratemeyer's novels filled a void that satisfied the longing for adventure and excitement felt by these teenagers.

At the time he began writing books, adult adventure and mystery novels were quite popular. He wrote twenty-two of the Nick Carter weekly dime detective stories in the 1890s, and their popularity led him to surmise, correctly, that what appealed to adults would also appeal to a younger generation. In the beginning, his novels were often simplified, non-violent versions of what the grown-ups were reading. He felt his series books were ideal for young readers: filled with familiar characters who are obviously good or bad; a style of writing that is easy to understand; and obvious clues (in the case of mystery novels) that help the reader feel he or she is solving the case along with the protagonist.

After Stratemeyer's death, Andrew Svenson, one of the Syndicate's partners, discussed the Syndicate's writing rules, including use of plot, characters and their personal-ities, and setting. He said the stories contained "a low death rate, but plenty of plot. Verbs of action, and polka-dotted with exclamation points and provocative questions. No use of guns by the hero. No smooching. The main character introduced on page one and a slam-bang mystery or peril setup. Page one is eighteen lines. The trick is to set up danger, mystery, and excitement there, on page one. Force the kid to turn the page."

All the books relied on action—and lots of it. The struggle between good and bad was central to the suspense that held the reader. The plot always included a discovery, the uncovering of secrets, chase scenes, spying, and sometimes kidnapping, but never killing. There was always lots of physical activity and excitement. Once in a while, the characters would be allowed a quick, chaste kiss, but romance was never a staple. At the end of every story, all loose ends were tied up neatly and any unanswered questions were answered. Heroes were rewarded for their good deeds, and those who harassed them were appropriately punished. Crime doesn't pay in a Stratemeyer novel.

No doubt some of the appeal of these series novels was the excitement the main characters always seemed to experience. Compared to the everyday life of real adolescents, these heroes' and heroines' lives were the stuff of dreams. According to Svenson, the leading characters are exaggerated, "extraordinary adolescents." Although not perfect, they seem to excel at whatever they try, are able to master any task, and face up to any challenge that comes their way. In the early series, the protagonists came in pairs: the Outdoor Girls or the Motor Boys, for example. Later, the heroes were more individualized: Tom Swift, Ruth Fielding, and Nancy Drew. In these latter books, the hero was always assisted by friends, supporters, and helpmates who were even more stereotypical than the main character: the good sport, the overweight dependable friend, and the clown. And it wasn't only the good guys who were stereotypically portrayed. The villains usually did not have redeeming qualities. Inevitably, though, they recognize and understand their faults when confronted at the end of the book.

From book to book, the characters' dialogue is similar and the leads have easily recognizable speech patterns. The supporting cast of characters also speak in a way that is typical for his or her "type." The protagonist's friends will often tell corny jokes or consistently exclaim using one particular word: "Yikes!" or "Holy catfish!" Regular characters are usually idiosyncratic, such as Mr. Damon in the Tom Swift series who routinely blesses every part of his wardrobe. The bad guys or lower-class characters are identifiable by their dialects. Stratemeyer novels are famous for their use of language and characterizations that today would probably be viewed as racist.

Main characters were developed with the same formulaic approach. Even the most tomboyish or liberated of heroines are often seen as gushing or using their feminine wiles to get their way. At the end of *Betty Gordon and the Mystery Girl*, "the protagonist rubs her cheek affectionately against her uncle's coat sleeve and says confidentially, 'I'm so happy . . . because every one else is happy!'" It's not only

Did you know...

Stratemeyer's protagonists were "wide-awake American boys" who *Smithsonian* called "superteens one and all" who "refused any reward, settling for lemonade or cookies."

Not everyone loved the Syndicate's series, however . . .

"But while teachers pushed Robert Louis Stevenson, the nation's juveniles hid Dave Fearless behind the covers of *Kidnapped*. Every year more books, more series, came out. Teachers grumbled and parents got together." *Smithsonian*, October 1992.

AND

From an editorial in the December 1905 issue of *Library Journal*: "Shall the libraries resist the flood and stand for a better and purer literature and art for children, or shall they 'meet the demands of the people' by gratifying a low and lowering taste?"

the girls who are melodramatic. In *The River Boys Winning a Fortune*, Dick Rover exclaims, "I'll tell you what— old friends are best! . . . Every one of them is sticking to us like glue!"

In Syndicate novels, mythical towns and locations were intertwined with real ones. When the Rover Boys weren't on the road, they were at home on Riverside Drive in Manhattan—a very real location. No matter the setting, the protagonists are able to get their work done unimpeded by adult intervention. Whether parents, teachers, or police— no one ever seems to bother the boy and girl sleuths.

Perhaps it was that lack of adult supervision that so bothered the adults who criticized Stratemeyer's work. For although young people bought and read his books by the thousands, parents, educators, clergy, and others were vocal in their opposition to the types of books the Stratemeyer Syndicate was publishing.

One of the criticisms had to do with the style of the novels. The use of an omniscient narrator who consistently breaks into the narrative served to slow the pace and interrupt the action. For example, in *Battling the Wind* in the Ted Scott Flying series, the pilot, Ted Scott, is losing control of his plane during a storm when the narrator says, "And so, while he is watching that awful plunge with the fear of impending death in his heart, it may be well for the benefit of those who have not read the preceding volumes of this series to tell who Ted Scott was, and what his adventures had been up to the time this story opens." If that narrative doesn't dampen the action, nothing will!

Billman writes that librarians, educators, and literary critics cite the problems with artificial constructions, syntax, and grammar found continually from book to book. This group felt that the Syndicate's books lowered children's literary tastes and expectations through their poor construction. A typical quote from one of the Rover Boys books serves as an example: "Dick! Dick! Are you killed?" In addition, Stratemeyer never had his characters "say" anything. According to the *Smithsonian* article, "For page after page, characters suggest, smile, remark, mutter, reason, muse, murmur, or ejaculate their words."

Other critics decry the racist and ethnic elements. Still others label the novels as sensationalist, trashy, and vulgar. Some librarians banned series fiction altogether. Some critics even blamed the rise in juvenile delinquency (another by-product of increased leisure time among adolescents) on Stratemeyer. One of the loudest critics was Franklin K. Mathiews, Chief Scout Librarian of the Boy Scouts of America, who called the Syndicate's books "racy, mile-a-minute fiction" and claimed the reading of these novels would damage boys' minds. Mathiews even went so far as to publish an article in *The Outlook* magazine titled "Blowing Out the Boys' Brains" in which he claimed these new series crippled boys' imaginations by their excessiveness. He wrote, "I wish I could label each one of these books: 'Explosives! Guaranteed to blow your boys' brains out.'" He went on to say that in these adventure books, "no effort is made to confine or control these highly explosive elements," i.e., craving for excitement and a passion for action and thrills. The result was that "as some boys read such books, their imaginations are literally blown out and they go into life as terribly crippled as though by some material explosion they had lost a hand or foot." He hated that the heroes of these books were able to overcome "difficulties and crushing circumstances as easily as in fairy tales."

Even as recently as the 1970s, criticism of the books

included statements such as "wooden," "escapist," and "regressive." As Billman notes, however, the irony is that these books were written from a conservative point of view. How is it then that they can be called "explosive" because of the superficial action scenes? Although some parents no doubt heeded the warnings of Mathiews and others, their children found ways around the critics—even if it meant hiding the most recent Stratemeyer offering inside a more "acceptable" book. And the kids continued to read.

By the late 1920s, the Stratemeyer Syndicate had firmly established itself. In 1926, Stratemeyer added Mildred Wirt to his list of regular contributors. She wrote numerous volumes in the Ruth Fielding series as well as the Dana Girls and Nancy Drew. Leslie McFarlane joined the Syndicate in that year as well, initially working on the Dave Fearless series. The Hardy Boys, one of the best-known boys' series ever, was launched the following year, with the bulk of the books written by McFarlane. Shortly after Charles Lindbergh made his solo flight across the Atlantic Ocean, Stratemeyer launched the Ted Scott Flying Stories, which was a hit and remained so throughout the Great Depression of the 1930s, one of a handful of series to do so.

On May 10, 1930, Edward Stratemeyer died at the age of sixty-eight after contracting pneumonia. Even though he outlined the first three books about a young, pretty, courageous young woman who would go on to bewitch generations of young readers, he died just after the first Nancy Drew book was published, never getting to experience the series' enormous success.

Speculation within the publishing world was that the Syndicate would unravel after Stratemeyer's death, but it did not—thanks to the dedication and hard work of his daughters, Harriet Stratemeyer Adams (who married Russell

After Edward Stratemeyer's death in 1930, his two daughters, Harriet (shown here) and Edna, took over the day-to-day operations of the Syndicate. Harriet faced criticism for rewriting and revising many of the old books in various series.

Adams in 1915) and Edna. Although Stratemeyer's wife, Magdalene, had legally inherited the business, she was ill couldn't manage it, and died in 1936.

Harriet explained, "They [the publishers] begged my sister and me to continue." The sisters took over the day-to-day operation of the Syndicate, with Harriet eventually writing some of the Nancy Drew books. Ironically, Stratemeyer had never allowed Harriet to write books for the Syndicate, even though she asked him repeatedly. He is reported to have told her that while his heroines might be permitted a career, real women belonged at home and that men were the providers. In a way, Harriet later complied with his request, moving the Syndicate offices near her East Orange, New Jersey, home, where she could keep an eye on her family while continuing to run the Syndicate in the manner her father had established. Although the number of series declined throughout the 1930s and '40s, she kept the most popular series alive—the Hardy Boys, Tom Swift, Bobbsey Twins, and Nancy Drew.

Edna Stratemeyer worked in the Syndicate office and created plot outlines for several series until she married Wesley Squier in 1937. She even wrote one or two volumes. In 1942, she moved to Florida with her husband and daughter. After moving, she still had input on major decisions, but Harriet took over total management of the Syndicate in partnership with several writers and editors.

By the 1950s, only a handful of successful series were still being produced by a handful of contributors. Tom Swift, Jr. was launched in 1954 and was written mainly by James Lawrence, a mechanical engineer who also wrote radio scripts. It was during this time that Harriet began a major revision project. Rewrites of earlier works were undertaken to eliminate ethnic stereotypes and update technology in order to keep readers interested. She was widely criticized for many of the rewrites, which included all the books in the Hardy Boys, Nancy Drew, and Bobbsey Twins series. According to a Website devoted to Edward Stratemeyer, all the books were shortened from twenty-five chapters to twenty, and some received entirely new plots. In addition to cutting the "outdated cultural references, she also deleted the detailed prose, interesting characterizations, and more leisurely pace of the originals. The results were mere skeletons of what had been before." Although Harriet was criticized for these revisions and for her (false) claim to be the "real" Carolyn Keene, author of the Nancy Drew series, she also was praised for her dedication to the Syndicate and the series books her father had so loved.

Edna died in 1974, the year before the final Syndicate series was launched. The Wynn and Lonny series, stories about racing, lasted only three years. Simon & Schuster won the rights to publish any new stories from Grosset & Dunlap in 1979 and bought the Syndicate outright in 1982, shortly after the death of Harriet at age eighty-nine.

THE ROVER BOYS
ON TREASURE ISLE

The
ROVER
BOYS'
SERIES

for
YOUNG
AMERICANS

BY ARTHUR M. WINFIELD

Launched in 1899, The Rover Boys was Stratemeyer's first series and laid the groundwork for the Syndicate's subsequent adventure series. Shown here is the thirteenth book in the series, The Rover Boys on Treasure Isle, *which was published in 1909.*

5

Heroes to Boys Everywhere

BY THE TIME Edward Stratemeyer developed the Rover Boys series, he had been writing for years. His adventure stories for children had been published in dime novels and magazines, but the Rover Boys, launched in 1899, was his first series, and by many accounts, his favorite. More than 5 million Rover Boys novels have been sold, and after his death, most obituaries noted that Stratemeyer's greatest accomplishment was the creation of that series.

The success of this series was unprecedented in juvenile literature. Its popularity grew for more than twenty-five years and continued in print after his death. The Rover Boys helped Stratemeyer perfect his formula, which he used later to find success with subsequent series.

In one of his introductory letters to the reader, Stratemeyer wrote, "To those who have read any of the previous volumes in this Rover Boys Series, the three brothers will need no special introduction. For the benefit of new readers, allow me to state that Dick was the oldest, fun-loving Tom next, and Sam the youngest. They were the sons of Anderson Rover, widower and rich mine owner . . . "

As *Smithsonian* wrote in 1992, Stratemeyer's formula "would define juvenile fiction for the next 50 years . . . suddenly 'rags-to-riches' was no longer the only dream. Adolescents trapped in a classroom, tenement or city yearned to journey to distant lands, go to college, toy with technology, play ball in the major leagues. And being adolescents, they wanted to do all this as if there were no such thing as parents."

The Rover brothers attended Putnam Hall, a military board-ing school, and later Brill College in the Midwest. They were described by Stratemeyer as being "lively, wide-awake American boys" and had a cast of supporting characters that included best friends, girlfriends, and villains. The first generation of Rover boys was the subject of twenty volumes, printed before 1916. The final ten books of the series were about the children of the original three and were called the Second Rover Boys Series. The four junior Rover Boys attended Colby Hall, run by a friend of their fathers, and managed to get into as many adventures as their fathers had.

Although the boys spend the appropriate amount of time in school, their adventures frequently take them out of the classroom to exotic locales. They spend time on a ranch, shipwrecked, and hunting. At every turn they were faced with villains: mysterious strangers whose devious plans were always thwarted by the brothers by the end of the book. The books themselves were suspenseful and melodramatic.

According to Billman, the Rover Boys series "originally depicted youthful adventures, games, and hi-jinks, but Stratemeyer soon introduced elements of melodrama and detective work." The boys often were on searches for missing people or buried treasure. They traveled to exotic locations, such as Africa in *The Rover Boys in the Jungle*, to try to find their missing father. In 1928, *Literary Digest* called their adventures "unprecedented." Even so, they invariably manage to defeat their enemies and escape whatever scrape they had managed to get themselves into. *Literary Digest* mentions one volume in which the brothers were caught in a burning cabin, while an avalanche was "rolling down on them from above" and the bad guys were shooting at them. However, "they would emerge unscathed, restore the missing fortune, be rewarded by three rousing cheers, and an arch look from Dora, Nellie, and Grace [their girlfriends] while the discomfited bullies, outwitted again, began plotting at once their future conspiracies, to be related in the next volume of the Rover Boys Series for Young Americans."

As the popularity of the Rover Boys grew, Stratemeyer concocted several new series, building on its success. He created new heroes, put them into unbelievable situations, and watched them grow. It was during this time that he talked his publishers into cutting the cover price for these novels in half, from a dollar to fifty cents. The price break allowed many more children to buy the books without having to ask their parents for money.

The Rover Boys series was unique in that it combined several elements not commonly found in adventure fiction for boys or men. Although these adventure stories routinely included travel and mystery, and the books often were set in a school of some sort, rarely did they include love interests.

But the three Rover brothers all had girlfriends, who they

met while at boarding school and later married. All three couples later lived in adjacent townhomes in New York City and had four sons among them who went on to follow in their fathers' footsteps. "The females in the Rover Boys books are not mere frills, as they are in later Stratemeyer Syndicate mysteries for boys," writes Billman. "Intrigues of a romantic nature provide actual subplots in a number of volumes . . . the ritual events of personal romance—namely, proposals, engagement announcements, and weddings—are given much space and weight in the scheme of these stories."

The second generation of Rover Boy detectives was launched in 1917 and ran until 1926. Stratemeyer balanced the series and perhaps kept it easier for the reader to keep track of all the Rovers running around by creating the children in the image of their fathers with the same personality traits. So, the eldest Rover Boy Jr., Jack, was born to Tom, the eldest Rover Boy, Sr., and exhibited the same leadership abilities. Dick, the middle original Rover, had twin boys, Andy and Randy, as energetic and mischievous as he. And Sam's son, Fred, was quiet and nondescript, just as his father had been. Two daughters were born to the original Rovers but were rarely mentioned. The second set of Rovers, likewise, all had long relationships with their girlfriends and surrounded themselves with signature and stereotypical friends, mostly there to provide comic relief between all the mystery and melodrama. Of course, there was a whole cast of villains: some worse than others, some who showed up book after book, and others whom the reader meets only once.

TOM SWIFT

While the original Rover Boys were attending Putnam Hall and solving all types of mysteries, Stratemeyer debuted a new type of hero: a different sort of leading character, and something of a departure from his previous works. Tom Swift was a young man who, according to his stories, invented most of the twentieth century's marvels, including television, the tank, and a photo telephone! His series debuted in 1910, and the thirty-eighth and final book was published in 1941.

The pseudonym used for the Tom Swift series was Victor Appleton, with Howard Garis being the primary ghostwriter. Tom Swift was described as an "inventor" but of so many varied objects that he was claimed "as one of our own" by groups from engineers to race car mechanics to pilots. His skill and unmatched imagination appealed to a wide audience and caught on with readers in a different way than the Rovers, the Hardy Boys, or Nancy Drew.

Keeline offers this explanation for the popularity of Tom Swift books: "The difference is that Tom seemed 'real'—an absurd notion, when you consider that his books, far more than Stratemeyer's other series, centered on technological inventions that did not yet exist. But the feeling of the series was real, because it appeared at a time when many Americans really had tested the boundaries of technology and pushed America rapidly into an age of mechanical marvels."

By this time, Alexander Graham Bell had made his first phone call, Thomas Edison had illuminated the world, and the Wright Brothers had flown with the birds—all "impossible" feats. Why not Tom? It has been acknowledged that the Tom Swift books aren't science fiction but are about legitimate, or quasi-legitimate, science. His inventions are all based on either real technological advances or on those that were imminent.

In typical Syndicate style, the Tom Swift series contained a regular cast of characters: Tom's friend Ned, "an upright young man"; Mr. Damon, "a clumsy eccentric with a good heart"; Mary Nestor, shy girlfriend and later wife; Eradicate Sampson, a stereotypical black servant; and Koku, a "loveable giant" whom Tom found and kept as a "Man Friday." In addition, Tom's father, also an inventor, appeared in nearly every edition.

The original Tom Swift had been out of print for nearly a decade when Harriet Stratemeyer Adams created a series about his son, Tom Swift, Jr. James Lawrence, a scientific writer, was hired to be the primary ghostwriter for this series which ran from 1954 to 1971. Like their predecessor, Tom Swift Jr. books reflected the technology of the time. "Where Swift senior had created planes, Swift junior created rocket ships," Keeline wrote. "Many of its thirty-three volumes focused on adventures in outer space."

A third Tom Swift series was launched in 1981 after the Syndicate had been bought by Simon & Schuster. This series lasted until 1984 and wasn't connected in any way to the first two series. He was simply another scientific adventurer and inventor who happened to have the same name. Finally, the fourth Tom Swift incarnation appeared in 1991 and concluded in 1993 after thirteen volumes. He wasn't so much of an inventor as a fighter of mutants, monsters, and cyborgs.

THE HARDY BOYS

In the mid-1920s, Stratemeyer decided to create a juvenile series fashioned after the adult mystery novels that were quite popular at that time. He wrote to Grosset & Dunlap, one of his main publishers:

> Detective stories are as interesting to boys as to grown folks. In this line I suggest two boys, Joe and Frank Hardy, the sons of a celebrated detective. From their father they hear of various cases and gradually start to solve the mysteries. They get onto the 'side issues' of the crimes . . . Thus while the father is the real detective, the brothers do their full share . . . their work as amateur detectives would furnish plenty of incident, exciting but clean.

Copublisher Alexander Grosset suggested to Stratemeyer that instead of beginning a new series with only the two Hardy Boys as lead characters, he should incorporate the brothers into a new series with several different heroes. Maybe he was afraid that juvenile mysteries wouldn't sell. Fans of the Hardy Boys can be grateful that Stratemeyer didn't listen to Mr. Grosset.

Did you know...

"We owe you and the others a great deal."

"All of you are regular heroes!"

"Heroes? Pooh!" sniffed Tom. "Nothing of the sort. We are just wide-awake American boys."

And they are wide-awake; aren't they, kind reader?
— *The Rover Boys on the River*

ADVERTISEMENT RUN BY GROSSET & DUNLAP

Q. "Have You Ever Thought Why You Get So Much Fun Out of Reading the Hardy Boys Stories?"

A. It's probably because the Hardy Boys, Joe and Frank, are fellows like yourself. They like action, plenty of it. They are as full of curiosity as a couple of bloodhounds. And just leave a mystery around and they'll be in it before you can say, "Sherlock Holmes!" And it's because they can drive a car and pilot a speedboat, are at home in the great outdoors, and keep their heads in an emergency. (And an emergency is always just around the corner.)

The Hardy Boys hit the scene in 1927. Leslie McFarlane, a Canadian journalist and freelance fiction writer, generally considered to be one of the Syndicate's best ghostwriters, was offered the chance to write the breeder volumes, which ended up selling so well. He was kept on as the main Hardy Boys writer and authored most of the books in the series. Although not an immediate success, the Hardy Boys eventually sold more than Tom Swift. As Billman writes, this was not bad for a series one critic called "nothing more than updated Rover." The Hardy Boys came on the scene at about the same time as several adult detective novels and owe a good deal of their success to that genre as a whole and to the boys' adventures series that came before them.

With only two boys to concentrate on, as opposed to the three Rover Boys, the characters became more fully developed. Unlike the Rovers and Tom Swift before them, the Hardy Boys don't age throughout the run of the series. They remain frozen in time as teenagers. Of course, they are much more mobile than the average teenager. Frank and Joe typically travel through their adventures in convertibles, but they also can be found on motorcycles, in boats, planes, and almost anything else that goes fast.

According to Billman, they "exemplify the juvenile mystery genre in bold and formulaic relief: the fast action of chases on land and sea and sometimes underground, the code-breaking and intrepid detectives, the stereotypical villains, the inescapable clues—the footprints are always fresh—and a secure if crime-ridden setting where justice surely triumphs and the hero is resoundingly commended by one and all."

The Hardy Boys series is a good example of how one of the longest-lasting Syndicate series had to change with the times in order to continue to attract readers. As American culture and tastes changed, so did the Hardys. When the series launched, the boys wore hats, ties, and sweater vests. By the 1970s, they had longer hair and wore less formal clothing. The stilted styling and often intrusive writing changed over the decades as well. In 1933, *Footprints Under the Window* ends with this sentence, "And have you guessed by this time, my readers, that the footprints under the window were those of the famous detective, Fenton Hardy?" This short ending was much different than Stratemeyer's earlier habit of spending half a page or more making sure the reader hadn't missed a beat. But even this limited aside made the reader aware of the story, rather than allowing him to become a part of it.

Regardless of the cultural updates, the basic Hardy Boys plot remained the same: fast-paced, remarkable detective work (especially considering they are teenagers solving adult-like crimes) and the triumph of good over evil.

In contrast to the Rover Boys, the female characters in the Hardy Boys series are never fully developed. Frank and Joe each have a girlfriend, but they are rarely seen and never—or hardly ever—change. Callie Shaw, "the object of Frank's affection" originally had brown hair that later changed to blonde. And Iola Morton, whom Joe calls "all right, as a girl" lost weight over the years. Even though the girls are bit players throughout the book, they are always on hand at the conclusion to congratulate their heroes. Another difference between the two series is the continuity in the villains seen throughout. In the Rover Boys, the bad guys returned in book after book, but new evildoers were introduced in each Hardy Boy volume.

The Hardy Boys series was set in Bayport, a small New England coastal town that had more than its share of negative occurrences. They use Bayport as a base from which to travel to exotic locations to solve mysteries. Each book in the Hardy Boys series followed a standard formula, according to Arthur Prager, in a 1971 article in the *Saturday Review*. First, their father Fenton gives them a case, or they become suspicious of someone new to Bayport. Then there is a "fortuitous coincidence," such as overhearing the villians talking about their evil plans. Next, the villains put the boys in danger. And finally, the boy detectives narrowly escape disaster through near miraculous intervention at the last moment. The author's pen name for this series was Franklin W. Dixon, and one of his trademarks was the use of several plot lines throughout the book. He kept readers not only guessing the outcome of each, "but the interconnection that will inevitably tie together the disparate threads," writes Billman. Sometimes the sense of mystery was heightened by frightening ingredients, and in later years, the stories contained elements of political intrigue.

Typical Hardy Boys adventures take place on islands and in caves and underground tunnels. Such places naturally evoke feelings of desolation and mystery; they're not places that are visited regularly. Frank and Joe were eternal adolescents, but it was an adolescence full of adventure, mystery, and admiration for their exploits, both from their fellow characters and their loyal readers. They solved the same type of mysterious adventures, getting into and out of the same seemingly inescapable situations and engendering the same support from every-one around them.

Several new series were created in the mid-1920s in addition to the Hardy Boys. Bomba the Jungle Boy, a jungle adventure series; Don Sturdy, an explorer adventure

The Hardy Boys first appeared in 1927 and became one of the Syndicate's most popular series. **The Flickering Torch Mystery** *was the twenty-second installment in the series which followed the adventures of teen detectives Frank and Joe Hardy.*

series; the Garry Grayson Football Stories, a sports series; James Cody's Ferris's X Bar X Boys, a western adventure series; the Nat Ridley Rapid Fire Detective Stories; and the Ted Scott Flying series. Ted Scott and Bomba both ran for twenty volumes, but the Hardy Boys was the decade's big winner.

The original Bobbsey Twins series holds the record for the longest running children's book series. Launched in 1904, the series consisted of seventy-nine volumes, the last of which was published in 1979. Shown here is The Bobbsey Twins Camping Out, *which was released in 1923.*

6

The Girls Join the Fun

EDWARD STRATEMEYER MAY not have believed in letting his daughters go out to work, but he placed no such constraints on the girls who starred in the eighteen series for girls that he conceived. In 1908, *Dorothy Dale, a Girl of Today* was the first to be published. She was followed in 1910 by the Motor Girls, who had been fashioned after the Motor Boys series. These travel adventure series set the stage for all the successful series of that genre that followed.

Although many of the girls' series have faded from memory— the Moving Picture Girls, the Girls of Central High, and the Outdoor Girls—a generation of young women was entertained by them just as the boys' series were keeping the boys occupied. Indeed, many of the girls' series launched by Stratemeyer were spin-offs of the boys' series or at least plotted out in the same way. This was Stratemeyer's method of operation: if a plot worked, use it again and again.

Most of the girls' series consisted of two main characters, and it wasn't until around 1930 that it became more common to find the protagonist acting alone. The Ruth Fielding series was an early exception to that rule of thumb.

RUTH FIELDING

Ruth Fielding was an orphan who, after getting the obligatory boarding school education, went to Hollywood where she became a celebrated playwright, actress, and detective. Unlike many of Stratemeyer's main characters, Ruth eventually married and had a child. Thirty volumes were published between 1913 and 1934 under the pen name of Alice B. Emerson, who later also authored the Betty Gordon series.

According to Billman, the Ruth Fielding series doesn't fit neatly into a specific genre. The first several books are about Ruth's school days. In the next several volumes, she is traveling. Then there are three books in which she is a Red Cross nurse. The final fifteen books in the series tell of her "skyrocketing career in the movie industry and of her personal growth from schoolgirl to single career girl to wife and mother." She adds that at least three-fourths of the series are mysteries. This changing style allowed Ruth to explore the many possibilities that were opening up to women of the early twentieth century. In addition to dealing with external situations, she is also constantly growing and learning within her personal life. Throughout it all, she maintained her old-fashioned morality in the changing world.

As with most other Stratemeyer characters, Ruth comes

from a small, nondescript town. She is orphaned at a young age and cared for by an uncle. And just like other Stratemeyer figures, Ruth is accomplished at a wide variety of endeavors: she is not only a prize-winning playwright, but she has studied Red Cross lifesaving, drives a car—fast— and flies her own plane. She is not overly romantic or "girlish." She likes to keep busy and enjoys mental challenges. According to Billman: "Ruth is no-nonsense, unsentimental, independent, aggressive, ambitious, and assertive." In spite of these attributes, she is "Victorian in her notions of women and family" and often worries about her husband, Tom, and what others think of her.

Unlike some of the boys' series, in which the villains were always male, the Ruth Fielding series boasts female "bad guys." Her enemies were often women who were jealous of her Hollywood success. Ruth had her friends as well. Her childhood friend and schoolmate, Helen, almost always accompanies her in her adventures, and Helen's twin brother, Tom, becomes Ruth's husband.

Unfortunately, after she got married, only seven more Ruth Fielding novels were published. At that point, the paradox of being a wife and mother who continued to work as a movie director and solve mysteries created too much of a conflict for the character. She began to seem unsure and cautious as her previously competitive nature diminished and she became more introspective. Her former free-spirited nature seemed reined in by marriage, as she often acted uncharacteristically subservient toward Tom. The confusion over gender roles that had been hinted at in earlier novels came to full bloom in the final volumes, causing readers to desert her. "No doubt Edward Stratemeyer wanted to portray a happy blend of the old-fashioned, family-oriented female in whom he believed and the new young woman on the go who would thrill readers," writes Billman. "Unfortunately the combination did not gel, and even Stratemeyer seemed aware of the incongruity." The books and Ruth lost direction and lost readers.

Perhaps it was this difficulty of a grown-up Ruth, who had to deal with the conflicts between a home life and one on the road, that caused subsequent series to freeze their main characters in time, so they never aged or really changed.

THE CORNER HOUSE GIRLS

The Corner House Girls series, written under the pen name Grace Brooks Hill, was a moderate success for the Stratemeyer Syndicate. Launched in 1915, it ended eleven years later. The four sisters in the series are Ruth, Agnes, Tess, and Dot Kenway. Ruth is the oldest at about eighteen. Dot is about five years old, and Agnes and Tess are somewhere in the middle. The girls are orphaned and destitute, and then they inherit money and a home on a corner—hence the name of the series—from an uncle. They live with their Aunt Sarah and two kind servants. With no real authority figures to limit them, the Kenway sisters experience some wonderful adventures.

Unfortunately, their adventures are as formulaic as most of the Stratemeyer series, even to the point of having the same or nearly the same titles as some of the others. But the girls were also "wholesome, flawless, and concerned with the good of others," with characteristics reflecting their individuality and, all in all, "an appealing and enjoyable series," according to Dr. Ilana Nash, a Syndicate researcher.

THE BOBBSEY TWINS

The Bobbsey Twins series holds the record for the longest-running series of children's books. Launched in 1904, this was the first "tots" series, written for young children of both sexes, and the first series issued by the new Stratemeyer Syndicate. Howard Garis and his wife Lilian wrote many of these volumes under the pseudonym Laura Lee Hope.

Like the Hardy Boys, the Bobbsey Twins aged only slightly over the years, and also like the Hardys, the Bobbseys underwent complete revisions in the mid-1950s. It was during these revisions that Harriet Stratemeyer Adams reacted to the criticism about the racial overtones in most of the series by editing most of them out, including the broad dialect used to depict the two black servants in the Bobbsey Twins books.

The Bobbsey family consisted of two sets of twins: Nan and Bert, who were older, and Flossie and Freddie, the younger pair. They lived in the upper-middle-class town of Lakeport with their parents and Sam and Dinah, the servants.

The twins and their family enjoyed "mild adventures" such as trips to innocuous places like the circus, beach, and country fair. In each novel, each new adventure was met with a wide-eyed innocence that echoed the nature of children in the early part of the twentieth century. Understandably, this endearing character trait lost favor by the 1960s and '70s.

In 1979, under new publisher Simon & Schuster, the original series was brought to a close at seventy-nine volumes and a new one launched in which the twins were a little older and more in tune with the times. This series ended after only fourteen volumes. Again, in 1987, a new Bobbsey Twins series was introduced and called, appropriately enough, "New Bobbsey Twins Series." This last attempt at chronicling the lives and adventures of the Bobbseys lasted about six years and thirty volumes.

Mildred Wirt, pictured here at 96, displays The Mystery of the Ivory Charm— *one of twenty-three books Wirt wrote in the Nancy Drew series. This Stratemeyer Syndicate heroine, who debuted in 1930, was so popular that she outsold the Hardy Boys and Tom Swift.*

7

Nancy Drew, Girl Detective

NANCY DREW IS arguably one of the most well-known young women in fiction. Millions of girls continued to read of her exploits long after her creator and his Syndicate were gone. The Nancy Drew series of mysteries were true detective stories with a different thrilling mystery solved in every volume. Conceived and outlined by Stratemeyer in 1929, the first three volumes were written by Mildred Wirt, a ghost-writer who was working on the Ruth Fielding series at the time. Initially, Stratemeyer felt that Mildred made Nancy too aggressive and fresh, but apparently Grosset & Dunlap disagreed, and published the first book in April 1930.

Tragically, Stratemeyer died a few weeks later, never seeing the unprecedented success the series would attain. The pen name Carolyn Keene was used by several writers including Wirt, who wrote twenty-three of the first thirty volumes.

There were valid reasons for Nancy's popularity. She was young, blonde, blue-eyed, beautiful, talented, smart, and good. Her bravery, resourcefulness, and independence awed even adults. Who wouldn't want to mirror those characteristics? *Smithsonian* wrote in 1992: "In her 1930 debut, Nancy Drew drives a convertible, pilots a speedboat, fixes a sprained ankle, repairs a motor, quotes Archimedes, and finds a missing will in an old clock. Such expertise quickly made the adventure series of this superteen the best-selling Stratemeyer work of all time, topping the Rover Boys, topping Tom Swift."

An indicator of Nancy's appeal was seen during the height of the Great Depression. During the Christmas season of 1933, Macy's department store in New York City sold 6,000 volumes of the series. Later, when smaller series were terminated because of the depression, Nancy continued. Likewise, she survived Harriet's rewriting fervor of the 1950s, the cultural shifts of the '60s and '70s, and continues to be popular with young readers today.

The Nancy Drew character and series met the same basic formula as other Syndicate series. She was young (eighteen), had few adult authority figures (her mother was dead), she lived with her indulgent attorney father and faithful servant in the town of River Heights, and was rich. She didn't work or attend school and had the freedom and money to travel anywhere she wanted while doing good deeds just for the heck of it. She never takes a misstep and is so consistently perfect that some have criticized her consistency, finding it boring. Everyone seems to agree that Nancy's close relationship with her father, Carson, is one of the reasons behind the series' success. He was everything one could want in a parent: warm, indulgent, respectful, and attentive, and one more reason young readers wanted to *be* Nancy.

As in all Stratemeyer series, Nancy has her group of regular friends who help solve mysteries and generally serve as foils for the hero or heroine. Nancy was no exception and was accompanied by her two best friends, female cousins named George and Bess. These girls had completely opposite personalities: George a tomboy, athletic but clumsy; and Bess graceful and sweet. Nancy's personality stood somewhere in between and shone through because of her friends' different personalities. Nancy also was given a "steady" in Ned, her constant boyfriend throughout the series. Nash says that Ned added "a dash of emotion to the books." For example, in *The Secret in the Old Attic*, a subtheme is Nancy's sadness because she thinks Ned has asked another girl to a dance. "This mushy stuff never ran away with the mystery narrative, but it gave at least a taste of humanity to Nancy, who had a tendency to seem robotic." Another humanizing factor was the addition of a pet. Nancy found a terrier in a park, took him home, named him Toto, and allowed him to accompany her on many of her adventures, where he often helped her sniff out the answers or nail the bad guys.

Girls' mystery series are a definite trend in literature, characterized by some of the same qualities contained in series books for boys. Nearly every book includes characters who never age or age gradually. All have a similar plot, and most of the series have characters who are not fully developed, even though they are in some way superior individuals: they are stronger, more beautiful (or handsome), or more intelligent than the average adolescent. Sometimes they are all three!

It is the formulaic nature of series books that attract adolescent readers who are trying to find their place in the world and where they fit into society. These books reassure the young reader that good will conquer evil, and the characters they have come to know and love will return again and again to provide them with unending thrills and adventures. In the introduction to *Nancy Drew and Company: Culture, Gender, and Girls' Series*, Sherrie A. Inness writes:

> The names of the heroines change; they drive different cars and pursue different adventures, but the plots are essentially formulaic. The leading character (with or without her pals) is remarkably capable, gorgeous, and far more intelligent than any adult. Because of her innate ability, this paragon is able to solve mysteries, fly planes, cure the ill, and perform many other exploits with incredible ease, not even breaking into a sweat. Although there are some variations to this dominant character, the heroines of girls' series are similar in many ways.

Girl series novels began to rise in popularity in the late 1800s, quickly gaining ground after the turn of the century. In the 1830s, Jacob Abbott, a Congregational minister, wrote a series for boys about a young boy who had some mild adventures, but he was always accompanied by an adult who would lecture on moral values and the importance of becoming a responsible adult.

The earliest dime novels, which appeared in the mid-1800s, were popular among both adults and boys for their stirring stories of the Wild West or big-city detectives and

The immediately popular Nancy Drew book series soon found its way to the big screen as Bonita Granville (second from left) starred in four Nancy Drew movies in the late 1930s, including **The Detective,** *which was based on the tenth book in the series,* **The Password to Larkspur Lane.**

other adventurous characters. Girls still were encouraged to read religious or domestic novels, which contained little or no excitement within their pages.

Shortly thereafter, the adventure quotient was raised by books written by William Taylor Adams under the pen name Oliver Optic, in which the heroes were unusually strong young men who could take on any contender.

Similarly, Horatio Alger wrote "rags-to-riches" books in which the heroes would endure great misfortune before they invariably were discovered to be the missing heir to a huge fortune or experienced some other fortunate accident of birth, making all their earlier struggles worthwhile.

Optic and Alger were Edward Stratemeyer's early role models, and although he expanded on their themes, his earliest series books contain much of the same plot devices as those who influenced him. The presence of girls in the books of the first two authors, however, was nearly nonexistent. They were there merely as "window dressing" to the boys as someone's mother or sister—or they existed simply to marry the hero. This wasn't so strange considering women's roles on the page were simply mirroring those of their counterparts in the real world at the time. Stratemeyer would expand the roles for women, culminating in one of the most widely read and beloved female characters in literature: Nancy Drew.

Researchers in the field of children's literature contend that the mystery novel is the favorite genre of both boys and girls. As previously mentioned, the style evolved from adult detective novels of the mid-to-late 1800s. Bobbie Ann Mason wrote in *The Girl Sleuth*, "While children's mysteries too stress a strong sense of justice and social order, they aren't whodunits—for murders are taboo—but adventures." The girls' books tend to be more "mysterious," relying heavily on "crooks and clues and gothic settings," while the boys' books rely on action.

As girls' series books grew in popularity after the turn of the twentieth century, their actions and freedoms in the written word reflected the growing restlessness of the overall female population in the real world. Stratemeyer's early girl detectives were liberated and heroic and became role models for generations of young girls. "These modern girls wore khaki knickers and climbed trees, rode horses and rowed boats . . . they often exhibited uncommon bravery and maturity . . . performed amazing rescues or revealed uncanny intuition . . . then at night, they danced," writes Mason. They were considered "liberated" for their ability to do what most women of the day couldn't, or at least weren't expected to do. In addition to their actions and abilities, they wore comfortable clothes and drove cars!

The mobility afforded by the driver's license gave these girls more freedom than most readers could imagine. It conferred a certain status on the heroines, and they appeared to be larger than life. Mason uses a passage from *The Outdoor Girls on Cape Cod* to illustrate the admiration felt by some of the Outdoor Girls' friends. (The Outdoor Girls not only drove around "casually" but also went hiking and camping on their own.)

> "Do you mean you drive around all alone?" she asked, her voice a little awed.
>
> "Suppose you have a blow-out?"
>
> "That's easy," laughed Mollie. "Ask us a hard one. If we have a blow-out or a puncture, we fix it, or use the spare."
>
> "Oh, but I think it's wonderful!" cried Irene, her Irish eyes sparkling and her face rosy. "Think of being able to go around like that in a motor car and have all sorts of lovely adventures! Do you belong to a club or something?"

The "liberation" of these early heroines was somewhat superficial compared to the later activities of Nancy Drew, for example. The earlier Stratemeyer series for girls focused on girls in groups. Yes, they could drive a car, sail a boat, and have various adventures, but they also relied on each other. They received money from their families, were interested in boys and romance, and performed less hands-on detective work. These were the days when women and girls were seen as "dainty creatures" in need of protection. While these girls were making the first tentative steps toward true liberation and equality, they still had a long way to go.

As Mason points out, Stratemeyer and other authors walked a fine line when introducing the more or less liberated young women to the world, writing, "It was risky to let a female strike out on her own—and succeed." The series form was based on continuing adventures, which called for independence, but in reality, there were few areas in which women were allowed the freedom to actually succeed independently. They had few legal rights and few roles outside the home. Writes Mason, "An extraordinary kind of heroine was required, one who would enthrall with her glamorously interesting life, but who would not, of course, encourage revolution."

She goes on to claim that these early mysteries tantalized girls, building the desire for adventure without threatening the comfortable advantages of femininity. The protagonists were helped by men and money, creating a comfortable paradox toward which the young reader could aspire: to be secure and safe, while having wonderful and remarkable adventures.

Gradually, groups of girls gave way to the single girl detective. Ruth Fielding came on the scene before Nancy Drew, but the conflict her character felt between her domestic home life (as a wife and mother) and her sometimes dangerous detective work transmitted itself to the reader. The series lost focus and eventually died out.

By the time Nancy came along, the public was ready for

a strong female who performed in a decidedly masculine way in a truly masculine profession, yet managed to exemplify all the feminine virtues of beauty, style, and glamour. While Nancy was primarily a detective, many of the girl series that were launched in response to her success featured girl detectives who did their sleuthing "on the side" and not as a primary occupation. Later on, some of the female characters were nurses, journalists, and even movie stars. Once the United States entered World War II and many women went out to work in previously all-male professions, the characters in girls' series grew as well.

Mason reminds us that readers of Nancy Drew books were never allowed to forget "that our heroine—gunning down the highway after a gang of crooks—is a sweet

Did you know...

"She was ahead of her time. She was not typical. She was what the girls were ready for and were aspiring for, but had not achieved.

Girls were ripe for a change in literature. They were way overdue for a good, entertaining story that broke away from the old style of writing. I think Nancy was the character the girls were waiting for. They were just waiting for someone to verbalize it.

She was an individual, from start to finish. . . . She was just a person who believed in her own freedom."

—Mildred Wirt, the original "Carolyn Keene," in a 1999 interview young lady who dresses nicely and enjoys having tea with little cakes." Nancy upheld a surely unattainable ideal of the perfect girl. She never lost her cool, even in the direst or most disturbing of circumstances. She is more mature than many 30-year-olds, even though she is 16 when the series starts and never ages past 18. She is always sweet, self-possessed and self-confident, serious, smart, courageous, kind, and mature. Although not really portrayed in many domestic situations, she nonetheless was capable of keeping a home. As noted in early books, she had lost her mother when quite young and managed her father's household for him almost single-handedly, with only a housekeeper to help out.

Through her superhuman abilities and accomplishments, Nancy has encouraged generations of young girls to believe in themselves, to believe that they can aspire to whatever they desire, and can achieve whatever they set their minds to. As Mason states admiringly, "She has made a daring stride into adulthood, and she also trespasses into male territory without giving up female advantages. Nancy's adolescent readers may not know whether to shave their legs and giggle to attract the boys they are discovering, or to join the boys' games and emulate them to win their approval, but Nancy does both; although she gives no thought at all to romance."

Nancy's two distinct personalities were characterized individually by her two sidekicks—cousins, Bess and George (who was female). Bess is passive, pudgy, and concerned with boys, makeup, and food. She is "squeamish, dainty, and feminine." On the other hand, George reflects Nancy's masculine side, with her short hair and repudiation of romance and romantic ideas. She is a tomboy who lacks grace and poise. Often, girls felt they had to be one way or the other, but Nancy made it possible to be well-rounded.

Bobbie Ann Mason wrote *The Girl Sleuth* in 1975 in the middle of the women's movement. In it, she discusses the impact Nancy Drew and other girl detectives had on adult women of that era and their growing feminism. She argues that the fact that these teenage girls had such unusual freedoms and were able to accomplish so much in a "masculine" domain was important to overall feminist consciousness. She is not the only researcher to write of the link and importance between Nancy Drew and the feminist movement.

Deborah L. Siegel's essay, "Nancy Drew as New Girl Wonder: Solving it All for the 1930s" and Sally E. Parry's "The Secret of the Feminist Heroine: The Search for Values in Nancy Drew and Judy Bolton" also discuss the paradoxes found in the Nancy Drew character and how these differences helped shape readers of the series. In addition, they investigate why the overall style remained so popular for decades.

Siegel's point is that Nancy "served as a bridge between the Victorian and the modern age." Although Nancy was seen as a modern girl, she held some very old-fashioned values. And it was precisely this paradox in her personality that helped her readers understand a changing world and figure out their place in it.

Parry makes the case for Nancy as a feminist who works hard to "restore the status quo and all that it implies about ideological, economic, social, and even gender relations." She looks for mysteries, often picking up those her detective father, Carson, is too busy to work on. And she reflects conservative values. She worked hard to help people, not just to reclaim their missing items, but by helping them emotionally when they were scared or insecure.

Parry continues: "Nancy Drew is a good feminist hero in that her role in these mysteries is a strong and active one. She often serves as a protector for orphaned children, helpless older women, or poverty-stricken older men. She is sometimes extraordinary. She's capable of driving automobiles, airplanes, and boats, as well as riding horses, playing golf, and swimming in an expert manner."

In *The Secret in the Old Attic*, Nancy takes the case over from her father and functions more or less independently thereafter, solving the mystery on her own. Yet she shows a traditional feminine characteristic when she cares for the granddaughter, and she accepts an evening gown as reward for solving the mystery—although as Parry says, "her true reward is increased fame and satisfaction that order and social hierarchy have been restored."

Although Nancy is a decidedly feminine character, her more masculine traits are often her saving grace. She moves about freely, has money to do as she pleases, is not overly involved with a family, isn't very interested in domestic matters, and enjoys her power and public recognition. Parry theorizes that Nancy was raised by her father "as the son he never had." This would help explain her masculine side. She also lacks any real female role model since her mother is gone, and the housekeeper is more of a servant than a mother figure.

Nancy was introduced in the early days of the Great Depression, and as Siegel argues, it's somewhat odd that she would have become so popular since she was from a solidly upper-middle-class background at a time when so many were struggling to put food on their tables. Nancy's adventures usually involve helping someone from the middle- or upper-class who has suffered some sort of a loss. Even when her clients aren't rich, they usually come from a privileged home, or are considered to be a "good" person. Invariably, the "evil" character is from a lower class or questionable background.

Nancy Drew possesses a strong belief in the distinctions between classes, believing that "those who succeed in a material sense are inherently better people." She judges others by their appearance, however, having a "good" or respectable background is more important than money, and she will be more indulgent of a poor person who carries themselves well and comes from a respectable background. Perhaps this was in deference to all those who had money but lost it in the stock market crash of 1929.

Coincidence plays a major role in the Nancy Drew books. Clues appear out of nowhere in pictures, old clocks, or within letters. Friends are always available to lend a helping hand or at least a sympathetic ear as Nancy attempts to sort out the pile of clues. Chase scenes and dangerous situations are standard. Nancy has been tied up and gagged, kidnapped, and locked up in a variety of places. Parry says Nancy's success "lies in being able to see what others fail to and in combining common sense with observation and intuition."

Sometimes Nancy disobeys the law in order to solve her mysteries. In many of the series books, authority figures—including the police and detectives—are shown to be unintelligent or even corrupt. However, she is straightforward and her choices are moral absolutes. She is able to bring order to chaotic situations, creating a sense of security. Even though she deals daily with rogues and horrible situations, she manages to retain and maintain her sense of innocence and belief that good will conquer evil and truth will prevail.

Stratemeyer's series books for young adults had long been belittled as "unacceptable" or "trash" by many educators and librarians, even as children everywhere clamored to read more of them. The fact that the Hardy Boys, Tom Swift, the Bobbsey Twins, and of course Nancy Drew have experienced such unparalleled success among the youth of the world should be validation enough. But now Stratemeyer's critics can be silenced once and for all. The fact that an early Nancy Drew novel, *The Mystery at Lilac Inn*, can be found alongside Thomas Jefferson's handwritten copy of the Declaration of Independence in the New York Public Library's Rare Books Division validates Stratemeyer's work in an unarguable way.

Siegel acknowledges that Nancy is not a timeless figure who is always interpreted in the same fashion. Instead, she is constructed and reconstructed by readers from different decades, with each generation bringing new considerations to bear on the girl detective's career as she adapts to the changing world. The Nancy Drew read by girls in the 1940s and '50s is now barely recognizable as the same person. As Siegel says, "her character has evolved to keep up with the times." Nowadays, Nancy wears an updated hairstyle and has aged in order to legally drive in every state. She also wears jeans instead of "sport dresses" and drives a blue Mustang convertible instead of a "roadster" of the same color. She is no longer confined to helping the unfortunate in River Heights and close to home but can chase international jewel thieves around the world.

Nancy came on the scene only ten years after women were first granted the right to vote and one year after the stock market crash of 1929. She offered escape to those suffering the harsh realities of the depression and exemplified qualities that were slowly recognized and acknowledged as acceptable and just by adults in the real world: the right and ability of women to be educated, financially independent, unmarried by choice, and powerful in areas outside the home. She can easily be seen as one of the first feminist role models.

Shaun Cassidy (left) and Parker Stevenson (right) played Joe and Frank Hardy, while Pamela Sue Martin (center) played Nancy Drew in The Hardy Boys/Nancy Drew Mysteries *television series that aired on ABC from 1977–79.*

8

The Stratemeyer Legacy

WHEN EDWARD STRATEMEYER first conceived of his literary syndicate, there was no way for him to know what the future would hold. He probably couldn't imagine the great success he was to achieve within the literary world. His innovative business plan, run of good luck, and fortunate timing took the publishing world by surprise. Millions read and enjoyed his work—even when they didn't know it was written, or at least plotted, by him. Beyond the written word lay a whole world within two mediums that hadn't even been invented in 1905.

Even Tom Swift, who "invented most of the technological

wonders of the twentieth century," may not have been able to foresee how the Syndicate's series would be advanced through the use of the new mediums of film and television. According to Keeline, both Edward Stratemeyer and Howard Garis, the principal ghostwriter of the Tom Swift series, "had a fascination with motion pictures . . . they were used both as a fictional plot element for this series and at least three other Stratemeyer Syndicate series."

One of the first Syndicate books to make the transition to the silver screen was *Carolyn of the Corners*. The book was produced as a silent film and starred Bessie Love as the orphan Carolyn. Unfortunately, as with most silent movies, no copies of this film exist today.

In 1938 and '39, four Nancy Drew movies were made—*Nancy Drew, Detective*; *Nancy Drew, Reporter*; *Nancy Drew, Troubleshooter*; and *Nancy Drew and the Hidden Staircase*, all starring Bonita Granville. Fan clubs grew up around these releases, increasing the popularity of the written versions.

From 1949 to 1955, eleven films based on the Bomba the Jungle Boy series were released starring Johnny Sheffield, who had played "Boy" in the Tarzan films. During the 1960s, Bomba was produced as a half-hour television series, keeping the character in the public eye for another generation.

In the 1950s, Walt Disney Studios created two short television shows based on the Hardy Boys mysteries. The first was developed from the first volume of the series, *The Tower Treasure*. About ten years later, a pilot was shown for a Hardy Boys series that never materialized. A few years after that a Hardy Boys cartoon show was introduced that lasted just one year. In it, the characters were in a rock band and solved mysteries in their spare time.

In the late 1970s, *The Hardy Boys/Nancy Drew Mysteries* television show debuted and lasted for two seasons. It was quite popular and generated a wide variety of products associated with the show. The two actors who portrayed Frank and Joe Hardy became true teen idols through this exposure. Parker Stevenson, who had acted in films before, and Shaun Cassidy, a pop music star, saw their careers take off. Pamela Sue Martin, who played Nancy, was a respected young film actress, and although the series stayed true to the books in many respects, viewers—driven in large part by the teenage girls who were attracted to the "Hardys"—simply didn't connect with Martin.

In the first season, the two shows alternated episodes, keeping the lead characters and their exploits separate. The Hardy Boys and Nancy Drew for the most part followed the plots and settings of their series books, with some minor character changes. In the second season, however, the three characters were combined into one show, angering Martin, Harriet Adams, and many fans. Near the end of the show's run, Martin left because

Did you know...

The Stratemeyer Syndicate came full media circle when, in 1978, two books were published by Grosset & Dunlap "based on the Universal Television series *Hardy Boys/Nancy Drew Mysteries* . . . based on the Hardy Boys books by Franklin W. Dixon and the Nancy Drew books by Carolyn Keene."

her character had become such a minor player. She was replaced by Janet Louise Johnson, a Hollywood newcomer.

The third season saw the show renamed *The Hardy Boys* and Frank and Joe were recast as United States secret agents who roamed the world solving mysteries. Romantic interests increased, the level of violence was raised, and the plots were written for more of an adult audience. These Hardy Boys were nothing like the boys of the novels. Each of these attempts to break into TV was accompanied by tie-in products including magazines, comic books, board games, lunchboxes, puzzles, posters, and Halloween costumes. Two records were even produced by the animated Hardy Boys band!

■　　　　　■　　　　　■

Beyond the short-lived successes of the television spin offs, Stratemeyer is still best known as the founder of the Stratemeyer Literary Syndicate and the author of the Rover Boys series. Many avid readers of some of the most popular books for adolescents don't know that Stratemeyer was the real Carolyn Keene, creator of Nancy Drew; the real Franklin W. Dixon, creator of The Hardy Boys; and the real Laura Lee Hope, creator of The Bobbsey Twins. As *Smithsonian* put it in 1992, he "was not a mere author; he was a literary machine. . . . Between 1900 and 1930 he turned his uncanny sense of young readers' tastes into an action and adventure factory that churned out more than 1,400 juvenile novels in 125 different series written under scores of distinct pseudonyms."

Stratemeyer's unparalleled success can be compared to the lives and adventures of some of his protagonists. Born to immigrant parents, he combined a sharp mind with an uncanny business sense and a knack for being in the right place with the right idea at the right time. He was said to be a strict parent: authoritarian but fair with his two daughters. He set up his Manhattan office not far from his home in New Jersey in order to spend more time with his family. His method of parenting extended to his office staff and cadre of ghostwriters, whom he kept on very short leashes. There were rules to follow if you wanted to work for Stratemeyer. And even the most onerous rule— one could never reveal his or her true identity as an author of any Syndicate books—didn't stop prospective writers from coming to him looking for work.

Smithsonian reported that Stratemeyer was able to create such believable juvenile characters because "when he sat down to write, his was a juvenile mind." The article claims

Did you know...

"As his gift to juveniles, Stratemeyer created the teen, 'wide-awake' boys and girls who could drive cars, fly airplanes, perform Houdini escapes, even quote Shakespeare. Orphaned or under the care of a single parent who was always out of town, Stratemeyer's superteens enjoyed unlimited freedom. In book after book, their mile-a-minute adventures sent them to camp, to the prairie, to college, to Mexico, the Pacific, the Rockies. Unlike the literature peddled by teachers, Stratemeyer's serial fiction was full of slam-bang action, cliff-hanging adventure."

—*Smithsonian* 1992

that he would don the persona of his leading character, staging mock shootouts in the office, or pretend to be Tom Swift stalking a lion. But when the book was finished, edited, and off to the publishers, Stratemeyer would again become the professional businessman.

Quite a few books have been published that explore the popularity of series books in general and those of the Stratemeyer Syndicate in particular. Young readers could identify with the characters in the stories. Even if their lives were not as adventurous or glamorous, the books seemed to say that if someone who faced so many hardships could succeed, become popular, solve mysteries, and travel to distant lands, so could they!

As Stratemeyer researcher Dr. Ilana Nash notes on her Website, ". . . he knew how to turn popular cultural trends into series books, most of which sold very well. This is what makes his body of work worth studying and collecting: It includes every conceivable subject that young people have found interesting. Its long success suggests that those topics remained attractive despite our century's many changes."

One lesson Stratemeyer learned early and well was that most profits in the sale of a book went to the owner of the copyright, not the author. For this reason, he made sure to retain ownership to all rights of his stories and those of his Syndicate, making him a rich man.

Although Stratemeyer seemingly had a magic formula for turning out one successful novel after another, there were many series that began and ended pretty quickly. Series such as Deep Sea, Speedwell Boys, or Boy Hunters simply didn't find an audience large enough to sustain their publication. Of course, the phenomenal success of many others—Bobbsey Twins, Nancy Drew,

Hardy Boys, and Tom Swift—overshadowed the fact that the lesser series even existed.

The Syndicate was not without controversy. Stratemeyer had plenty of critics of both his literary style and content. Although Stratemeyer's style could be cumbersome at times—especially when he interrupted the action to directly address the reader—and unremarkable in his choice of language, it was somehow comforting to a reader to have these familiar characters with all their idiosyncrasies—and those of the author—to come back to again and again. His faithful readers knew just what to expect when they opened one of his series books.

After his death, Harriet and Edna Stratemeyer managed to run the family business well, and increase its importance and product base over the next fifty-two years. They were very successful at continuing existing series, dreaming up new story lines and characters, expanding their distribution, dealing with publishers and ghostwriters, and eventually selling rights to TV and film. In the New York City Public Library archives, evidence is overwhelming of the impact Syndicate books had on American culture of the time. A synopsis of some of the archival material states: "News clipping scrapbooks offer a cross-section of the popular and critical response to Stratemeyer volumes. Dozens of fan letters from young readers testify to the broad appeal of Syndicate publications, while business correspondence and screenplays reveal how Stratemeyer characters achieved even greater popularity by their portrayal in television programs and in movies."

Some controversy continued to swirl around the Syndicate after Stratemeyer's death. Harriet Stratemeyer Adams claimed for a long time that she was the only author of the Nancy Drew books: the "real" Carolyn Keene. Other ghostwriters contributed to this popular series, of course, including the most prolific, Mildred Wirt. Harriet did, however, write the outlines for most of the books, edited them, and ultimately controlled all the plot developments in the series.

In 1979, Harriet Stratemeyer Adams signed a contract with Simon & Schuster, ending her long association with Grosset & Dunlap. The latter sued Adams and the Syndicate, unsuccessfully, for breach of contract. Shortly after Adams' death in 1982, the Syndicate was bought outright by Simon & Schuster, which donated a large collection of archival material to the New York Public Library.

The series of the Stratemeyer Syndicate have been called 'organic' in that they tend to take on lives of their own once they are launched into the public realm. Billman calls this tendency a "kind of literary Darwinism—a continuous process of creation, adaptation, and survival of the fittest." Of course, the revisions and adaptations of Harriet Adams during the 1950s helped create a contemporary feel for the books, even as they aged. New volumes were published with main characters who had undergone subtle and sometimes not so subtle changes to hairstyle, clothing, and even mannerisms and language. But changing with the times seemed to work as characters like Nancy Drew maintained a place in the hearts and bookshelves of America's youth.

In 1971, Arthur Prager wrote in the *Saturday Review*, "If anyone ever deserved a bronze statue in Central Park, somewhere between Hans Christian Andersen and Alice in Wonderland, it is Edward Stratemeyer, incomparable king of juveniles."

Today readers still live vicariously through the characters created by Stratemeyer. They are envied for their everlasting childhood and the adventures that make real life disappear for a while. Collectors and scholars and a whole new generation of adolescents can still find intrigue and adventure in the pages of a Stratemeyer Syndicate novel.

1862 **October 4** Edward Stratemeyer is born in Elizabeth, New Jersey, to German immigrant parents.

1877 He publishes a four-page booklet called *That Bottle of Vinegar* and a thirty-two page booklet titled *The Tale of a Lumberman*. He also wrote and published some of his first short magazine stories around this time.

1889 Edward sells his first substantial story, "Victor Horton's Idea," for which he receives $75 from the Philadelphia boys' magazine, *Golden Days for Boys and Girls*.

1891 Edward opens a stationery shop in Newark, New Jersey, while continuing to write and publish short stories. He also marries Magdalene Baker Van Camp during this year. Shortly thereafter, his father dies.

1892 The Stratemeyer's first daughter, Harriet, is born.

1894 Edward's first book, *Richard Dare's Venture*, is published by Merriam. He also works as an associate editor of *Young Sports of America*.

1895 The couple's second daughter, Edna, is born.

1896 Edward sells his stationery store and begins his own story paper, *Bright Days*.

1898 He sells the first book in his Old Glory series. *Under Dewey at Manila, or The War Fortunes of a Castaway* was highly successful partly because its plot mirrored newspaper headlines about The Spanish-American War.

1899 Edward's fortunes are on the upswing as he introduces the Rover Boys Series for Young Americans written under the pseudonym Arthur M. Winfield. He also completes several unfinished projects started by his childhood "heroes" Horatio Alger, Jr. and "Oliver Optic" the pen name of William Taylor Adams.

1904 Edward introduces his longest-running series, The Bobbsey Twins.

1905 He formally organizes the Stratemeyer Literary Syndicate and opens an office in Manhattan.

1910 Tom Swift debuts, written mainly by ghostwriter Howard Garis

1926 Edward hires two writers who will prove among the most prolific within the syndicate. Mildred Wirt writes many of the Ruth Fielding books, then goes on to write most of the Nancy Drew volumes as well. Canadian journalist Leslie McFarlane begins his stint with the Syndicate writing the Dave Fearless series. He goes on to write the Hardy Boys series.

1927 The Hardy Boys series is launched and assigned mainly to McFarlane. Eventually it becomes tied with Tom Swift for the best-known boys' series of the century.

1930 **April** The Nancy Drew series debuts and is written primarily by Mildred Wirt under the pseudonym Carolyn Keene.

1930 **May 10** Edward Stratemeyer dies suddenly after a case of pneumonia. Harriet and Edna take over the running of the Syndicate.

1982 The Stratemeyer Syndicate is bought by Simon & Schuster Publishers.

Because there have been so many volumes written for the various Stratemeyer Syndicate book series, it is difficult to pick out a few that are the "most popular" and give a plot description that is wholly unique to a particular book. Instead, here is a list of some of the early books and their real-life authors associated with their respective series.

According to Stratemeyer scholar James D. Keeline, the first fifty-eight books in the Hardy Boys series, beginning with *The Tower Treasure* in 1927 and ending with *The Sting of the Scorpion* in 1979, are considered to be the original books of this series. Collectors prize those written before the 1960s because they were published in hard cover with dust covers, and they were longer and written at a higher grade level than those that came later. All were published under the pseudonym Franklin W. Dixon.

Leslie McFarlane, a Canadian journalist and author, wrote the bulk of the Hardy Boys volumes including the first eleven. These were *The Tower Treasure*, 1927; *The House on the Cliff*, 1927; *The Secret of the Old Mill*, 1927; *The Missing Chums*, 1928; *Hunting for Hidden Gold*, 1928; *The Shore Road Mystery*, 1928; *The Secret of the Caves*, 1929; *The Mystery of Cabin Island*, 1929; *The Great Airport Mystery*, 1930; *What Happened at Midnight*, 1931; and *While the Clock Ticked*, 1932.

Mildred Wirt was a journalism student at the University of Iowa when she applied for a job with the Stratemeyer Syndicate. She first wrote a volume in the Ruth Fielding series for Stratemeyer which apparently pleased him, as he next asked her to write the first three volumes in the Nancy Drew series. Even though Stratemeyer felt Wirt had made Nancy more aggressive and brash than he had intended, the publisher liked her work, and Wirt continued to write volumes in this series under the Carolyn Keene pseudonym. In fact, she wrote twenty-three of the first thirty volumes in the series.

The first three Nancy Drew volumes were *The Secret in the Old Clock*, *The Mystery of Lilac Inn*, and *The Bungalow Mystery*, all published in 1930. The last volume Wirt wrote in the series was *The Clue of the Velvet Mask*, published in 1953. In between, she also wrote the following: *The Secret at Shadow Ranch*, 1930; *The Clue in the Diary*, 1932; *The Secret in the Old Attic*, 1944; *The Whispering Statue*, 1937; *The Mystery of the Brass Bound Trunk*, 1940; and *Clue of the Broken Locket*, 1934.

Howard Garis, best known for his Uncle Wiggily books, was the primary ghostwriter of the Tom Swift series, published under the pseudonym Victor Appleton. Three of the last books in the original Tom Swift series are considered highly collectible today. They are *Tom Swift and His Giant Telescope*, 1939; *Tom Swift and His Magnetic Silencer*, 1941; and the last title, *Tom Swift and His Planet Stone*, 1941.

The first fifteen books in the series were published in three years. In 1910: *Tom Swift and His Motor Car*, *Tom Swift and His Motor Boat*, *Tom Swift and His Airship*, *Tom Swift and His Submarine Boat*, and *Tom Swift and His Electric Runabout*. In 1911: *Tom Swift and His Wireless Message*, *Tom Swift Among the Diamond Makers*, *Tom Swift in the Caves of Ice*, *Tom Swift and His Sky Racer*, and *Tom Swift and His Electric Rifle*. In 1912: *Tom Swift in the City of Gold*, *Tom Swift and His Air Glider*, *Tom Swift in Captivity*, *Tom Swift and His Wizard Camera*, and *Tom Swift and His Great Searchlight*.

Laura Lee Hope was the pseudonym under which thirteen authors wrote the Bobbsey Twins series. It has been speculated that Stratemeyer wrote the first three volumes in the series, although they aren't written in his usual style. It is known that Howard Garis wrote most of the books in the early part of the series' run. Harriet Stratemeyer, Edward's daughter, and Lilian Garis, Howard's wife, also wrote many volumes.

The first Bobbsey Twins volume, *The Bobbsey Twins* or, *Merry Days Indoors and Out*, was published in 1904 by Mershon. Three years passed before the next volume was printed. *The Bobbsey Twins in the Country* was published in 1907 by Chatterton-Peck, as was *The Bobbsey Twins at the Seashore*. Soon, the Bobbsey Twins found a permanent home at Grosset & Dunlap, which published the series for more than seventy years. The next several volumes were *The Bobbsey Twins at School*, 1913; *The Bobbsey Twins at Snow Lodge*, 1913; *The Bobbsey Twins on a Houseboat*, 1915; *The Bobbsey Twins at Meadow Brook*, 1915; *The Bobbsey Twins at Home*, 1916; *The Bobbsey Twins in a Great City*, 1917; and *The Bobbsey Twins on Blueberry Island*, 1917.

THE HARDY BOYS SERIES

Written by Leslie McFarlane under the pseudonym Franklin W. Dixon

The Tower Treasure (1927)

The House on the Cliff (1927)

The Secret of the Old Mill (1927)

The Missing Chums (1928)

Hunting for Hidden Gold (1928)

The Shore Road Mystery (1928)

The Secret of the Caves (1929)

The Mystery of Cabin Island (1929)

The Great Airport Mystery (1930)

What Happened at Midnight (1931)

TOM SWIFT SERIES

Written by Howard Garis under the pseudonym Victor Appleton

Tom Swift and His Motor Car (1910)

Tom Swift and His Motor Boat (1910)

Tom Swift and His Airship (1910)

Tom Swift and His Submarine Boat (1910)

Tom Swift and His Electric Runabout (1910)

Tom Swift and His Wireless Message (1911)

Tom Swift Among the Diamond Makers (1911)

Tom Swift in the Caves of Ice (1911)

Tom Swift and His Sky Racer (1911)

Tom Swift and His Electric Rifle (1911)

THE BOBBSEY TWINS SERIES

Under the pseudonym Laura Lee Hope

The Bobbsey Twins or, Merry Days Indoors and Out,
   Edward Stratemeyer (1904)

The Bobbsey Twins in the Country, Lilian Garis (1907)

The Bobbsey Twins at the Seashore, Lilian Garis (1907)

The Bobbsey Twins at School, Howard Garis (1913)

The Bobbsey Twins at Snow Lodge, Howard Garis (1913)

The Bobbsey Twins on a Houseboat, Howard Garis (1915)

The Bobbsey Twins at Meadow Brook, Howard Garis (1915)

The Bobbsey Twins at Home, Howard Garis (1916)

The Bobbsey Twins in a Great City, Howard Garis (1917)

The Bobbsey Twins on Blueberry Island, Howard Garis (1917)

NANCY DREW SERIES
Written by Mildred Wirt under the pseudonym Carolyn Keene

The Secret in the Old Clock (1930)

The Mystery of Lilac Inn (1930)

The Bungalow Mystery (1930)

The Secret at Shadow Ranch (1930)

The Clue in the Diary (1932)

Clue of the Broken Locket (1934)

The Whispering Statue (1937)

The Mystery of the Brass Bound Trunk (1940)

The Secret in the Old Attic (1944)

The Clue of the Velvet Mask (1953)

THE HARDY BOYS

Frank and Joe Hardy were fashioned by Stratemeyer after the adult mystery novels popular in the mid-1920s. The brothers' adventures exemplified the juvenile mystery genre through their action scenes, code breaking, stereotypical characters—villains as well as "good guys"—and more than anything else, the ultimate triumph of good over evil.

NANCY DREW

Probably the most well-known young woman in fiction is Nancy Drew. She was popular among adults as well as adolescents for her many wonderful qualities. She was young, blonde, blue-eyed, beautiful, talented, smart, and good. In addition, she was brave, resourceful, and independent. Nancy was expert in everything she tried and displayed positive qualities young girls couldn't wait to read about and model.

TOM SWIFT

Tom Swift debuted in 1910 and was popular through the final book of the first series, which was published in 1941. Tom was more of an adventurer and inventor than strictly a detective. He appealed to his young readers for his skill, innovation, and imagination.

THE BOBBSEY TWINS

The Bobbsey Twins series was launched in 1904 and ended in 1992, making it the longest-running children's book series. The two sets of twins, Nan and Bert, the eldest, and Flossie and Freddie, the youngest, were upper-middle-class suburbanites who lived fairly settled lives with their parents and two black servants. The stereotypical way the servants, Sam and Dinah, were portrayed in the Bobbsey Twins books and the backlash against such racism was the catalyst that forced Harriet Stratemeyer Adams to revise her major series, a process that lasted several years and affected the Nancy Drew and Hardy Boys series as well.

The Bobbsey Twins was written for a younger audience—they were Stratemeyer's first "tots" series—and because of this involved "mild adventures": no car chases and kidnappings, but rather trips to the beach or county fair.

Billman, Carol. *The Secret of the Stratemeyer Syndicate: Nancy Drew, The Hardy Boys and the Million Dollar Fiction Factory*. New York: Ungar Publishing Company, 1986.

Dyer, Carolyn Stewart and Nancy Tillman Romalov, eds. *Rediscovering Nancy Drew*. Iowa City: University of Iowa Press, 1995.

Hedblad, Alan, ed. *Something About the Author*, Volume 100. Farmington Hills, Mich.: Gale Group, 1999.

Inness, Sherrie A., ed., *Nancy Drew and Company: Culture, Gender, and Girls' Series*. Bowling Green, Ohio: Bowling Green State University Popular Press, 1997.

Mason, Bobbie Ann. *The Girl Sleuth*. Old Westbury, N.Y.: The Feminist Press, 1975.

Stratemeyer Syndicate Records. Manuscripts and Archives Division, The New York Public Library, Astor, Lenox and Tilden Foundations.

Watson, Bruce. "Tom Swift, Nancy Drew and Pals All Had the Same Dad." *Smithsonian*, October 1992.

The Unofficial Stratemeyer Syndicate Homepage. *www.stratemeyer.net*

The Stratemeyer Syndicate on Keeline.com. *http://www.keeline.com/StratemeyerSyndicate.html*

Bloom, Clive, ed. *Stories and Society: Children's Literature in its Social Context*. London: Macmillan, 1992.

Dizer Jr., John T. *Tom Swift & Company: "Boys' Books" by Stratemeyer and Others*. Jefferson, N.C.: 1982, McFarland & Co.

Garis, Roger. *My Father Was Uncle Wiggily*. New York: McGraw-Hill, 1966.

Johnson, Deidre. *Edward Stratemeyer and the Stratemeyer Syndicate*. New York: Twayne, 1993.

McFarlane, Leslie. *Ghost of the Hardy Boys*. New York: Two Continents, 1976.

Plunkett-Powell, Karen. *The Nancy Drew Scrapbook: 60 Years of America's Favorite Teenage Sleuth*. New York: St. Martin's Press, 1993.

The Stratemeyer Syndicate on Keeline.com.
   [http://www.keeline.com/StratemeyerSyndicate.html]

The Unofficial Stratemeyer Syndicate Homepage.
   [www.stratemeyer.net]

page:

10: Stratemeyer Syndicate Records, Manuscript and Archives Division, The New York Public Library, Astor, Lenox and Tilden Foundations

16: From *Golden Days for Boys and Girls* (2 Nov. 1889): 769, "Children's Literature Research Collection," The Philadelphia Free Library

24: Syracuse University Library, Department of Special Collections

36: Stratemeyer Syndicate Records, Manuscript and Archives Division, The New York Public Library, Astor, Lenox and Tilden Foundations

45: Beinecke Rare Book and Manuscript Library, Yale University

48: Courtesy Matt Leonhard

59: Frontispiece "The Hardy Boys Were Stunned by What They Saw!" illustrated by Paul Lane, from *The Flickering Torch Mystery* by Franklin W. Dixon. (Hardy Boys Mystery Series ®) ©1943, © renewed 1971 by Simon & Schuster, Inc. Hardy Boys and all related characters and images are copyright and registered trademarks of S&S, Inc. All rights reserved.

60: Reprinted with the permission of Simon & Schuster Children's Publishing Division from the frontispiece "A Fire was built in front of the tent to make the place more cheerful" by W.S. Rogers from *The Bobbsey Twins Camping Out* by Laura Lee Hope. ©1923 by Simon and Schuster, Inc. Bobbsey Twins is a registered trademark of Simon and Schuster, Inc.

66: AP/Wide World Photos

71: Photofest

82: © Bettmann/CORBIS

Cover: Stratemeyer Syndicate Records, Manuscript and Archives Division, The New York Public Library, Astor, Lenox and Tilden Foundations

BRENDA LANGE has been a journalist, author, and public relations professional for more than fifteen years. During that time, she has written for newspapers, magazines, and trade publications, and performed public relations functions for various non-profit agencies. She received her bachelor's degree from Temple University in Philadelphia and is a member of the American Society of Journalists and Authors, National Writers Union, and International Women's Writing Guild. This book is her second for Chelsea House Publishers. Brenda lives in Doylestown, Pennsylvania, with her husband and their children.